Love Poems

Love Poems

Dante Alighieri

Translated by
Anthony Mortimer and J.G. Nichols

ALMA CLASSICS

ALMA CLASSICS LTD
London House
243–253 Lower Mortlake Road
Richmond
Surrey TW9 2LL
United Kingdom
www.almaclassics.com

This edition of Dante's *Love Poems* first published by Alma Classics in 2014
The translations from *Rime*, *Vita Nuova* and *The Divine Comedy* first
published in separate volumes by Alma Classics in 2009, 2011 and 2012
respectively.

Translations © the translators, as indicated at the end of each poem
Extra material © J.G. Nichols
Notes © Anthony Mortimer and J.G Nichols

Printed in Great Britain by CPI Group (UK) Ltd, Croydon, CR0 4YY

ISBN: 978-1-84749-345-3

Contents

Love Poems

FROM
Rime

[I]

Dante da Maiano to other poets*

Wise man, regard this vision with some care,   I
And draw out its true meaning, if you please.
So here it is: a lady who is fair,
A lady whom my heart is keen to please,
Made me a present of a leafy crown
And placed it on my head invitingly;
And then I found myself wearing a gown
Made to her measure, so it seems to me.
And then, my friend, it was that, growing bold,
I took her gently in a fond embrace;   10
She did not struggle, no: she smiled at me.
I kissed her many times, and she just smiled:
I'll say no more – she made me swear to this.
My mother, who is dead, was standing by.

[J.G.N.]

[I a]

Dante Alighieri to Dante da Maiano

You could work out the meaning on your own,   1
You who are so renowned for being wise;
And so I shall reply as best I can,
Without delay, to your well-fashioned phrase.
Now true desire, so hard to satisfy,
Produced by virtue or by beauty, must –
So I imagine in my friendly way –
Be shadowed by the gift you mention first.
And by the gown, you may be sure, is meant
That she will love you whom you most desire;   10
Of this you have a clear presentiment:
I'm thinking of what happened next with her.
And by the figure of one dead is meant
The constancy you may expect from her.

[J.G.N.]

6

[II]

Dante da Maiano to Dante Alighieri

To find its value by experiment,   I
The goldsmith puts his gold into the fire
And, by refining it, he can be sure
Whether it's worth a little or a mint.
And I, to put my singing to the test,
Put it to you, the recognized touchstone
Of all who make this serious skill their own,
Or are reputedly among the best.
And I ask this, in my best poetry:
Will you, with your extensive knowledge, deign   10
To say what are Lord Love's most deadly cares?
I have not set my heart on splitting hairs
(Not something that you set your heart upon),
But ask what my worth is, what it will be.

[J.G.N.]

[II a]

Dante Alighieri to Dante da Maiano

Whoever you are, it seems to me you wear   1
A cloak of wisdom, one that is not light;
So that, because I cannot praise aright,
Or fairly answer you, I blaze with ire.
So be assured (I know myself) compared
With yours my wisdom is a grain of sand;
Nor do I take wise ways like you, my friend,
Who seem so wise, looked at from any side.
But, since my mind is what you would discover,
I shall without a lie make it quite plain,   10
And talk like someone talking to a sage;
So in all conscience here's what I allege:
Whoever is in love, with no return,
Bears in his heart a grief that's like no other.

[J.G.N.]

[III]

Dante da Maiano to Dante Alighieri

All you have said, so elegant and certain,   1
Exemplifies what people say of you;
And, what is more, we'd find it a great burden,
Trying to give the praise that is your due.
For you have risen to such high repute
No one can reckon it sufficiently;
And now whoever speaks of your estate
And thinks to praise it, simply speaks awry.
You say: to love when love is unreturned
Is the worst fate that can befall a lover: 10
And many say there's something worse than that.
And so I beg: be not too disinclined
In all your wisdom to again discover:
Is this truth from experience, or not?

[J.G.N.]

[IIIa]

Dante Alighieri to Dante da Maiano

Although, my friend, I do not know your name,   1
Nor even where he's from, whom I hear speak,
I do know that his wisdom has such fame
That nobody I know enjoys the like.
With men it is not hard to recognize
If wisdom's there – speech makes it obvious.
Since I'm obliged to send you nameless praise,
My tongue has much ado to talk of this.
Friend (I am sure of this, since I have known
True love), he feels most anguish, be assured,   10
Who is in love, but not loved in return;
That pain is worse than any other pain,
And that is why it is all sorrows' lord:
And hence comes every grief love can contain.

[J.G.N.]

[IIIb]

Dante da Maiano to Dante Alighieri

Alas, the grief that grieves me now the most   1
Is giving thanks, not knowing in what wise;
It needs, instead of me, someone as wise
As you, who lay uncertainties to rest.
The grief which you say many people suffer
Comes from your disposition, not from theirs;
These nuances are what my mind desires,
Being at the end, so often, of its tether.
I ask you in your wisdom to repeat
Your argument, and cite authorities   10
To make your thesis still more glorious;
It will be clearer if you answer thus,
And we'll be sure what brings most miseries,
Having the proofs that make it definite.

[J.G.N.]

[IV]

Dante da Maiano to Dante Alighieri

Love makes me love and suffers no distraction;   1
He has me so subjected to desire
That my poor heart cannot for one short hour
Send its thoughts in a different direction.
I have been trying hard to find out whether
Ovid's prescription's valid for love's cure,*
And as for me I find him but a liar;
So I surrender and beg grace and favour.
And now I really know and know for sure
That Love is not thrown back by strength or art,   10
Or wit or any words that may be found:
There's only pity and the skill to endure
And serve him well: for so one plays one's part.
Tell me, wise friend, if what I say is sound.

[J.G.N.]

[IV a]

Dante Alighieri to Dante da Maiano

Knowledge and courtesy, shrewdness and skill,   1
Beauty, nobility, and affluence,
Strength of mind, mildness, sparing no expense,
Courage, worth – joined or individual,
These graces and these virtues everywhere
Overcome Love because they give such pleasure;
One may indeed be stronger than another,
But each will be contributing its share.
So, if you really wish, my friend, to use
A natural power or one that you have learnt,   10
Loyally use it for Love's delectation,
Not to oppose his gracious operation:
Against Love you will be quite impotent,
If you and he should ever come to blows.

[J.G.N.]

[V]

If, Lippo, it is you who are my reader,   1
Before you start to ponder
Over these words which I intend to say,
According to his wish who wrote to me,
I give myself to you,
And send such greetings as will give you pleasure.
Then I implore you, on your honour hear,
And hearing bring to bear
All your intelligence and your full mind:
I say I am a humble sonnet, and   10
I come and take my stand
In front of you, to make sure that you hear.

I come companioned by a naked maid*
Walking, but somewhat bashfully, behind:
She dares not wander round,
Because she has no clothes in which to hide;
I beg your gentle heart to take in hand
To clothe her,* and you two be close allied,
Till she is recognized
And where the fancy takes her walks around.   20

[J.G.N.]

[VI]

I beg Love to commend 1
My humble heart that he has given to you,
And I beg Mercy too
To make sure that you keep me in your mind;
I've hardly left behind
Your virtue and immediately I find
How I draw comfort from
The hope I nourish of returning home.
I shall but be a little time away,
Or so it seems to me, 10
And dwell continually
On how I see   your semblance in my mind;
When near, when far, when wandering to and fro,
My lady, I commend myself to you.

[J.G.N.]

[VII]

Relentless memory, that is always   1
Looking towards a time that now is past,
Is striking at my heart upon one side;
And amorous desire, that gently draws
Me to the precious region I have lost,
Assaults upon the other with Love's forces;
Nor do I feel I have enough resources
To fight off these attacks for very long,
Madonna, if you do not send me succour:
And therefore, if you ever   10
Think it your duty to deliver it,
Be pleased to send your greeting to my heart:
That may revive its strength and comfort it.

Be pleased, my lady, to provide relief
In this emergency for my poor heart:
It hopes for help from you and none but you;
A good liege-lord will never slacken off
When speeding to his vassal in distress,
Safeguarding him and also his own honour.
And certainly I feel the greater dolour   20
When I recall, my lady, how you stand
Depicted there within by Love's own hand;
Which means you ought to lend
Your hand to care more often for my heart;
For He by whom all good's apparent here
Holds us, since we're His image, the more dear.

If what you wish to say, my dearest hope,
Is that I should postpone what I am asking,
My answer is: I can no longer wait;
My strength is gone; I've almost given up;   30

16

Which ought to be apparent from the fact
That I am driven to this last resort:
A man should bear all weights – except the weight
Which has the power to crush him unto death –
Before he puts to proof his greatest friend:
How can he know what mind
He'll find him in? And if it turns out badly,
There's nothing costs so much and out of hand
Brings him to such an acrimonious end.

And you alone are she whom I most love,   40
Who can give me the greatest gift of all,
And she in whom my greatest hope is placed;
To serve you is the reason why I live,
And only things redounding to your honour
Meet my desires: everything else I loathe.
You can give me what no one else can give,
And all my thoughts are balanced in your hand,
Placed there by Love; of which I rather boast.
The reason for my trust
Lies in the kindliness of your demeanour;   50
For everyone who sees you sees indeed
From outward looks what pity is inside.

It's time now for your greeting to set out,
And come inside my heart that has been waiting,
My gracious lady, as you have been told;
But you should know the entrance to my heart
Is locked and barred and bolted by that arrow
Love shot the very day that I was stricken;
And so to go in there is now forbidden
Except to messengers from Love, who can   60
Open it by the will that shut the door:
And therefore in my war
Your greeting when it came would do me harm,

17

If it arrived here unaccompanied
By messengers from Love who is my lord.

Canzone, you must travel at full speed,
Since you know well what little time is left
To achieve the end for which you're on the road.

[J.G.N.]

[VIII]

These eyes of mine could never make amends for   1
Their dreadful lapse, unless they were to choose
To blind themselves: they saw the Garisenda
Tower* which affords us such entrancing views,
And failed to recognize (so curse them ever!)
The noblest lady known throughout that place:
So everyone must understand I never
Intend to treat with them and make my peace.
It came to this: that what they should have known
Without their sight, and come to understand,   10
They failed to notice when they saw; this is
The dreadful lapse which makes my spirits groan;
And I tell you, unless I change my mind,
I shall kill them, those ignoramuses.

[J.G.N.]

[IX]

Guido,* could some enchantment bring together   1
Lapo* and you and me under a spell,
And put us in a little boat to sail
What seas we chose in any wind whatever!
With neither stormy times nor evil weather
To hinder us or cause the slightest harm,
Our wills, a single will now, would become
One firm desire – to sail such seas for ever;
With Monna Vanna, Monna Lagia* then,
And her I listed as the thirtieth lady*   10
Transported too by Merlin the magician;
Love the sole topic of our conversation;
The ladies would all three be very happy,
And we, I'm sure, the happiest of men.

[J.G.N.]

[X]

There is a garland I   1
Have seen, such that henceforth
All flowers will make me sigh.

I saw, my lady, how you wore
That fragrant garland of fresh flowers,
And over and around it saw
One of love's little angels, singing
A subtle song which said:
"Whoever looks on me
Is bound to praise my lord."   10

If I should find that I am where
Fioretta, little flower, can hear,
I shall explain to her my lady
Wears all my sighs upon her head.
But, to increase desire,
My lady will appear
Crowned by the hand of Love.

These few unusual words of mine
Weave a *ballata* out of flowers,
Taking, to make themselves more graceful,   20
Clothing* from other hands than ours:
And so, I beg, for all
Who come to sing it, make
Your welcome cordial.

[J.G.N.]

[XI]

That lord, *Madonna*, living in your eyes,   1
So splendid that he is all-conquering,
Gives me great certainty
That you will be a friend and sympathize,
Since there where he elects his dwelling-place,
Bringing such beauty in his company,
He draws all that is good
Towards himself, fount of activity;
And so I add some comfort to my hope,
Which has been so beset and battle-tossed   10
It might well have been lost
If Love did not, against
All such adversities, give it great power
With his appearance and the memory
Of that sweet place and of that sweetest flower
Which with its lively colour
Circles my memory,
Thanks be to you and to your courtesy.

[J.G.N.]

[XII]

Violetta, you suddenly appear   1
Before my eyes, and in the guise of Love!
Pity, I beg, the heart that you have wounded,
Which, as it hopes in you, dies in desire.

Violetta, in more than human shape,
You kindled fire within this mind of mine,
Such the beauty I saw;
And, by the fiery spirit's act, you then
Created hope, which heals me partially
Whenever you smile at me.   10
Forget I turn to hope so trustingly,
And look at the desire with which I burn,
For many ladies tardy to respond
Have felt the pain of others' misery.

[J.G.N.]

23

[XIII]

Now turn your eyes and see who draws me on,   1
Meaning I must forgo your company;
Treat him with all due honour: this is he
Who, with his noble ladies, martyrs men.
Pray that his power, which kills not angrily,
Will let me come with you on some occasions:
For I tell you that how he frames his actions
Is understandable by all who sigh.
He came into my mind with might and main,
Depicting there a lady, one so noble   10
I throw all my resources at her feet;
And then he let me listen to a gentle
Voice: "Would you, and for nothing in return,
Send such a lovely lady out of sight?"

[J.G.N.]

[XIV]

I beg you, Love, let us exchange a word,   1
As a distraction from this fuss and bother;
And if each wishes to delight the other,
Let's take our lady as our theme, my lord.
The journey certainly will seem much shorter,
With such amusements to make time run on,
And I foretell a jubilant return,
With so much talk and yet more talk about her.
Begin now, Love: the moment's opportune
For you to start to show the reason why   10
You condescend to bear me company,
As my reward or out of courtesy;
My mind already lays its burden by,
Being so anxious that you should begin.

[J.G.N.]

[X V]

Barking of dogs, and hunters' hounding cries,   1
Hares breaking cover, shouts from those nearby,
Impetuous greyhounds suddenly set free
To race across the meadows, veer and seize!
Such are the very things which give delight
To one devoid of amorous intent;
But I, whom love's perplexities torment,
Find out while hunting one insistent thought
Which takes upon itself to tease me thus:
"So this is what you mean by gallantry –   10
Neglecting, for an uncouth sport like this,
The ladies and their fabled loveliness!"
Afraid that Love will hear what's said of me,
I fall a prey to shame and great distress.

[J.G.N.]

[X V I]

The more Love beats you with his bunch of sticks,   1
The more you should obey and not resist.
Better advice than this, I must insist,
Cannot be found. Now anyone who likes
This word, take it to heart. He will apply
In time the remedy for your affliction,
Because the ills of Love weigh not a fraction
Of all his good. Your heart must pave the way
For following him; he will be at the height
Of his great power, if he has stricken you   10
As you declare in those fine things you write;
And as you follow, do not go askew
One jot, for he alone can give delight,
Granting his faithful servants all their due.

[J.G.N.]

[XVII]

My sonnet, when Meuccio's* pointed out,   1
Greet him the instant that you are in sight,
Then throw yourself down running at his feet,
So that it's clear you know what's fit and right.
And when you have been there a little while,
Don't be afraid to greet him once again,
And state the business you've been sent upon,
First making sure you draw him to one side;
And say: "Meuccio, he who is your friend
Sends you some things of his which he holds dear,*   10
Hoping they'll bring him closer to your heart."
Then make sure that you give him for a start
These (they are brothers of yours), and make them swear
To stay with him and never be returned.

[J.G.N.]

[XVIII]

See from my lady's eyes a light appear,   1
So noble that, where it is visible,
The things it shows are indescribable,
Because they're so exalted and so rare;
And from their rays upon my heart there pours
An influence that makes me quake in fear
And say: "I never want to come back here" –
But that's beyond the limit of my powers;
And I go back to where I was subdued,
Encouraging my eyes to face their fear: 10
They first experienced this enormous might.
My eyes are shut, alas, when I get there;
Desire which leads them on has been destroyed:
So Love must make provision for my state.

[J.G.N.]

[XIX]

Into your hands alone, my noble lady,   1
I commend my spirit in its dying throes:*
It is so full of suffering as it goes
That even Love, dispatching it, feels pity.
So closely did you bind it to its lord
That it was quite incapable of more
Than telling him, whatever he wanted, "Sir,
Do unto me according to your word."*
I know that you hate anything unjust:
So dying now, which I do not deserve,   10
Means all this bitterness inside me grows.
My noble lady, now while I still live,
And for my comfort as I sink to rest,
Do not be niggardly: delight my eyes.

[J.G.N.]

[XX]

I feel this pity for myself so deeply   1
I suffer just as much
From sympathy as from the martyrdom;
Painfully and dejectedly, alas,
I sense against my will
The air which will compose my last sigh come
Into this heart her lovely glances wounded
Once Love with his own hands had split it open
To bring me to the instant of destruction.
How sweet, O misery,   10
Gentle, and kind, they raised themselves to me,
When starting me upon
This road which leads to death in such distress,
And said, "In our light you will find your peace."

"We shall bring your heart peace, and you delight,"
This lovely lady's eyes
Used to say once upon a time to mine;
But, after she had come to understand
That by her power alone
I had been robbed already of my mind,   20
Under Love's banners her eyes turned right round;
And so the sight of her victorious
Never appeared again, not even once:
Which means my soul is left
In sadness, which expected consolation,
And now at its last gasp
It sees the heart to which it once was bound,
Which, still in love, it has to leave behind.

In love and full of tears it fades away,
Leaving this life behind,   30

31

Disconsolate: Love sends it on its way.
And as it goes it mourns so grievously
That when it's not quite gone
Its Maker pities its great misery.
It has withdrawn inside the heart, with all
Of life that still remains to be extinguished
Only with the departure of the soul;
There it complains of Love,
Who is expelling it beyond this world;
It folds in close embraces   40
The spirits that all weep continually
Because they are to lose its company.

The image of this lady is still reigning
Within my memory,
There where she was enthroned by Love her guide;
Untroubled by the trouble she can see,
She seems more beautiful;
More and more happily she seems to smile,
Raising her homicidal eyes and crying
Upon the soul that weeps upon its way: 50
"Now, wretch, it's time you went: do not delay."
The image of my desiring
Cries out like this as always, even though
The grief she brings is less,
Since all my feelings must perforce decrease
As I draw near to where all woes will cease.

The day that lady came into the world
(If we trust what we find
In memory's book which now has almost failed)
My little body was subjected to   60
A strange unwonted passion,
So terrible it left me full of fright;
All of a sudden all my faculties

Were in abeyance and I fell to earth,
Stricken by light that struck into my heart:
If this book does not err
My life itself was seized with such a shudder
It even seemed that death
Had come into this world and come for it:
But He Who made the world now pities it.   70
When all that loveliness appeared to me
To give me so much grief
(Noble ladies to whom I have been speaking),
That faculty which is the major one
Seeing the fount of pleasure
Became aware its trouble had begun;
It recognized all the desire created
By the attentive gaze she forced on me;
It wept and told each other faculty:
"Her image will appear   80
In all its beauty, and not whom I saw,
Which fills me full of fear;
She will be lady over all of us
The instant that her eyes decide on this."

It is to you, young ladies, I have spoken,
Whose eyes have beauty for their ornament,
Whose minds are overwhelmed by love and stricken:
I want these words of mine
To be commended to you everywhere:
And in your sight I pardon   90
That lady for my death brought on by her,
Which she has never shown compassion for.

[J.G.N.]

[XXI]

The grievous love that is conducting me   1
Deathwards – responding to the will of her
Who once maintained my heart in happiness –
Has taken, and is taking day by day,
Out of my sight the light of such a star
As I could not believe would bring distress:
The wound, once hidden, that she gave to me
Is now revealed through overwhelming pain
Born out of that great blaze
Ending my joyful days,   10
So that I look for nothing now but ill:
And all my life (what little life remains)
Will sigh until my death-day saying this:
"I die for her whose name is Beatrice."

That name, so sweet, which makes my heart so bitter,*
Will, every time I chance to see it written,
Renew the wretchedness from which I suffer;
And out of all this misery my body
Will grow so gaunt, my countenance so drawn,
I shall be fearful just to look upon.   20
And then no breath of wind will be too light
To bear me here and there till I am chilled;
Then I shall drop down dead
And my grief shall be led
Off by the soul as it departs in sadness;
And they shall be together ever after,
Recalling all the sweetness of her face
Which makes a nothingness of Paradise.

Considering all that I have found through loving,
My soul does not ask any other pleasure,   30

And does not dread what troubles lie in wait;
For, once my earthly body is worn out,
Love that has so disturbed me will depart
With her to Him Who understands it all;
And if God does not pardon her her sins,
She will be given a torment she deserves,
But with no dread of it:
She will so concentrate
Upon the image that drove her away
That there will be no pain which she can feel; 40
So, if down here she has had no reward,
Love will provide it in the other world.

Death, you who act to do this lady's pleasure,
Have pity and, before you ruin me,
Go to her and explain
How those bright shining eyes which sadden me
Have in this way, and to my loss, been taken:
If someone else is basking in their light,
Tell me about it lest I be mistaken,
And I shall die less troubled than I might. 50

[J.G.N.]

35

[XXII]

I saw some ladies in a noble band,   1
This feast-day of All Saints that is just past;
And one stood out from them as clearly first,
And Love was visible at her right hand.
Her eyes were throwing forth a ray of light
Looking most like a spirit formed of fire;
And when I was so daring as to stare
Into her face, an angel shone in it.
On all those worthy she bestowed her greeting,
Instinct with saving kindness and well-graced,   10
Until their hearts had virtue in repletion.
I think she was a lady out of heaven,
And she came down to earth for our salvation:
And that is why those near her can be blessed.

[J.G.N.]

[XXIII]

Where are you coming from, and why so stricken?   1
Kindly explain it all to me, I pray you:
I have a strong suspicion that my lady
Is sending you away in such affliction.
I beg you, noble ladies: don't refuse
To pause a little while upon your road
And to indulge this wretched fellow, stirred
To hear about his lady and her news,
Even though hearing be a heavy matter,
Since Love has banished me so utterly   10
That all his actions make the wound more bitter.
Look at me hard: see how I fade away,
And how my lowered spirits start to scatter
If, ladies, you neglect to comfort me.

[J.G.N.]

37

[XXIV]

"Ladies who manifest such sympathy,   1
Who is this lady who is so prostrate?
Can it be she who's painted in my heart?
Oh, if it is, don't hide the truth from me!
She is to all appearance so distressed,
Her countenance so altered and so pale,
She does not seem to represent at all
That lady who made other ladies blessed."
"Now if you fail to recognize our queen,
Who is so overcome, that's no surprise,   10
For what occurred with us was just the same.
But if you only look upon her eyes
And how they move, you'll recognize her then:
Don't weep – already you are scarce alive."

[J.G.N.]

[X X V]

Melancholy came up to me one day;   1
"I wish to be with you a while," she said;
And it appeared that when she came she had
Dolour and Grief to keep her company.
"Now go away, away!" is what I said;
There was a Grecian pride in her replies;
Then while she talked to me, quite at her ease,
I looked and saw Love coming, and Love had
Himself arrayed in unaccustomed black,
And his head covered too: he was a mourner;   10
Tears of sincerity streamed down his cheek.
I had to beg him: "Tell me what's the matter."
And he replied: "I am possessed by grief:
Our lady's in her death-throes, my dear brother."

[J.G.N.]

39

[XXIX]

You with the ability to speak of Love,   1
Hear my *ballata*: it is pitiful,
And speaks of one who is so powerful
That in disdain she's snatched my heart away.

She's so disdainful of the onlooker
She forces him to lower his eyes in fear,
Since always there is circling her own eyes
A halo formed of horrid cruelties;
And yet those eyes enclose the attractive figure
Of Love, making the noble soul cry: "Mercy!"   10
This image is so strong that, when it's seen,
It cannot but draw sighs from everyone.

She seems to say: "I shall not sympathize
With anyone who looks into my eyes,
Since in them I contain that noble lord
Whose arrows have struck home to me inside."
And certainly I think she keeps them hidden
So she alone can see them when she wishes,
The same way as a modest lady does
Seeing her own reflection in a glass.   20

I have no hope that she will ever deign
To cast a pitying glance at anyone:
In all her loveliness she is so fierce
Because she feels Love living in her eyes.
And yet, however much she keeps him hidden,
I still at times have glimpses of salvation,
Because my strong desires will act with vigour
Against that high disdain which makes me shiver.

[J.G.N.]

[X X X]

Since Love has now abandoned me for good,   1
Not as I would,
Since I had never been so full of joy,
But out of sympathy
And pity for my heart,
Which meant he could not bear to hear it weeping;
I shall direct my love-abandoned song
Against the wrong
Habit we've taken up of labelling
Something that's low and crude   10
To make it seem a good,
And call it charm, a thing so fine and fair
He's like an emperor
With an imperial cloak in whom it rules;
It is the perfect sign
Denoting virtue in its true domain;
Which makes me sure, if I defend it well
And show I understand it,
Love will afford his grace to me again.

Some men believe to throw their goods away   20
Is the best way
To win a place with all those worthy men
Who after death live on
And flourish in the minds
Of such as have a genuine understanding.
But good men do not like to see such waste:
They think it best
To hold on to the goods that would be lost,
Adding to their delusion
And that of all those people   30
Whose judgement in this matter is wrongheaded.

Who would not call it stupid
To gorge and guzzle and indulge in lust?
To preen oneself and prink
As though one were for selling in a mart?
The wise do not esteem a man for dress,
Which is an outward thing,
But for his wisdom and his noble heart.

And there are others always full of laughter:
What they are after   40
Is only to be considered as quick-witted
By those who are deluded
When they see others laughing
At things their own blind minds can't understand.
They use the most affected words and phrases,
With airs and graces,
Content to be admired though from a distance;
They never love a lady
Whose heart is given to loving;
Their conversation sparkles emptily;   50
They would not ever be
Inspired to woo the ladies with some charm,
But, like a thief to thieve,
They rush to snatch at some unseemly sport;
And not because behaviour that is charming
Is now so lost to ladies
That they're like animals without a thought.

Although the disposition of the stars
Is such that charm
Has gone away, and farther than I've said,   60
Yet I, who know it truly –
Thanks to a noble lady
Who demonstrated charm in all she did –
Forbear to hold my tongue upon this theme:
That would be wrong,

And place me with the enemies of charm;
So from this instant on
In much more subtle rhyme
I'll tell the truth, but do not know to whom.
Therefore I swear, by him   70
Who is called Love and brimming with salvation,
That none may win true praise
Unless his habit is to do what's good;
So, if my subject matter is to please,
As all men say it is,
It must either good or close allied.

This attribute is not a simple good,
Since it's denied,
Or blamed at least, where virtue is most needed –
In those most dignified   80
In the religious life,
In those whose disposition is to learning.
If charm is valued in a gentleman
It must be one
With other qualities, and this is why
It suits one person well
And suits another ill,
While simple virtue is for everyone.
There does exist a pleasure
That's consonant with love and good behaviour: 90
Those three together rule
And, ruling, they preserve the life of charm;
Just like the sun, which is a combination
Of its heat and its light
And of its perfect and attractive form.

In all things charm resembles the great star:
For, from its rising
Until it sets and hides itself away,
Its brilliant beams pour in

Their life and power down here   100
As matter is disposed to welcome them;
Just so does charm – disdainful of all those
Who seem like men
Externally, yet do not bear the fruit
Their leaves suggest they ought,
Because of evil ways –
Give good things also to the noble heart,
Being swift to vivify
With gracious looks and still more gracious ways
Which seem but newly born,   110
And swift in giving virtue by example.
O self-styled gentlemen, vicious and liars,
The enemies of charm,
Charm which is like the prince of all the stars!

The man of charm will give and will receive,
And never grieve
More than the sun in lighting up the stars
And welcoming their aid
To have its full effect:
For both of them all this is a delight.   120
He is not roused to anger by men's words:
He only heeds
Those which are worth the hearing, while his own
Are fine and full of charm.
He is held dear, and his
Company sought by people who are wise;
As for the uncultured crowd,
He rates their praises as he rates their blame;
No honours make him proud,
However high he is; but when there's need   130
To demonstrate his spirit, how it's free,
Well there he does win praise.
Those now alive do just the contrary.

[J.G.N.]

[XXXI]

My words who wander all the world about,   1
You who were born when I composed the line
(Honouring her who caused me so much pain):
"Angels revolving the third sphere with thought",*
Now go to her, since you are well acquainted;
Cry out to her to listen how you suffer,
And say to her: "We're yours, but you will never
From now on find our number is augmented."
Do not stay there: Love does not live with her;
But wear sad clothing as you move about,   10
The same sad clothing your old sisters wore.
And when you find one lady who is dear,
Then throw yourself down humbly at her feet,
Saying: "You are the one we should revere."

[J.G.N.]

[XXXII]

Sweet rhymes,* who always talk to one another   1
Of her who honours all, a noble lady,
One* will arrive, perhaps is there already,
Of whom you will declare: "This is our brother."
Do not pay any heed to what he says –
I beg by him who makes all ladies love –
Because in what he tells you there can live
Nothing that's any friend to truthfulness.
And if you were induced by words from him
To go to meet that lady who is yours,   10
Then do not stop, make sure you come to her,
And say: "*Madonna*, our arrival is
To recommend to you one plunged in gloom
Who asks: 'Where can I find my eyes' desire?'"

[J.G.N.]

[XXXIII]

Two ladies in my mind and at its height   1
Have come to words, with love their argument:
Urbanity and love's esteem are blent
In one where dignity and prudence meet;
The other dwells with beauty and delight,
And both adorned by her nobility:
And, thanks to my beloved master,* I
Throw myself down, a subject, at their feet.
Beauty and Virtue both address my mind;
The question is: can anyone remain   10
Between two ladies with his love unstained?
The fountain of fine speech says in his turn
That Beauty may be loved for pleasure, and
Virtue be loved for what it can get done.

[J.G.N.]

[X X X I V *]

"I am a young girl, lovely and a marvel,   1
And have come here to show to men on earth
Some beauties of the place that gave me birth.

I came from heaven and there I shall return,
Delighting with my light the souls above;
The man who looks on me and does not burn
Will never have the mind to compass love;
For there is nothing fair He failed to give
Who granted Nature the full gift of me
And placed me, ladies, in your company.   10

There is no star that does not share its light
And power with these eyes; my beauties are
A marvel to the world, for from the height
Of heaven they came down and from afar;
Knowledge of them cannot be found save where
There lives a man who in himself knows truly
How Love makes entrance through another's beauty."

These words all men may read upon the face
Of the young angel here revealed, and I
Who gazed on it so fixedly to trace   20
Her form more truly, now am like to die;
For when I boldly looked her in the eye
I felt the wound that never lets me cease
From weeping, and since then I have no peace.

[A.M.]

48

[X X X V]

Because you see yourself so young and fair   1
As cannot but wake Love within the mind,
Your heart has turned to hardness and to pride.

Proud you have made yourself and hard to me,
For now you seek my death; and I believe
You do it only from the urge to see
Whether Love has the force to take a life:
You find me, more than other men, your slave,
And so you care not for the pains I prove.
Now may you feel at last the power of Love!   10

[A.M.]

[XXXVI]

Who without fear will look into the eyes   1
Of this young lovely girl, for to a state
She has reduced me where I can await
Nothing but death, whose bitterness I taste?
See then how cruel is the lot that lies
Heavy on me, my life is singled out
As an example to show forth the fate
Of men who dare to gaze upon her face.

This is the end that I was destined for,
Since it was fit one man should be undone   10
And die that others might the danger shun;*
And thus, alas, I was so swift to draw
Life's contrary to myself, as from afar
A pearl attracts the influence of a star.*

[A.M.]

[XXXVII*]

Love, you send down from heaven above your might   1
As does the sun its splendour,
For where the objects that its beams encounter
Are noble, there its influence grows strong;
And just as it dispels the cold dark night,
So you, high master,
Drive from the heart all fierce choleric humour,
For nothing base resists your strength for long:
From you alone, Love, every good must spring
For which the whole world strives and suffers so;   10
Without you there is no
Good we might do that is not rendered vain,
Like some fine painting, darkly set apart,
That undisplayed remains,
Giving no joy with colour or with art.

As stars are struck by beams sent from the sun,
Your light still strikes my heart
Unceasingly, since from the very start
My soul became a servant to your might;
Thence a desire is born that leads me on   20
With speech's gentle art
To gaze on lovely things that, as their part
Of beauty greater is, give more delight.
My mind has been, through gazing on such sights,
Made captive by a woman young and fair
Who lit a fire there,
As water through its clearness kindles flame;*
Because, as she reflects on me your rays,
O Love, when she first came,
They all rose up, returning to her eyes.   30

As in her being she is beautiful,
Noble in bearing, fit to love,
So restless thoughts with no less grace revive
Her image in my mind where she abides:
Not that the mind itself is capable
To grasp so high a thing; but, Love,
From you the mind derives its strength to move
Beyond the skill that Nature has supplied.
Her beauty proves the virtue that resides
In you, if one can judge by the effect   40
Upon a fitting object,
As fire points towards the sun, its source;
Nor does the fire give or take that power,
But simply makes the force
More clearly seen through its effect elsewhere.

O Lord, whose nature is so nobly made
That all nobility
On earth, and every goodness that might be,
From your high majesty have taken start,
Regard my life and see how it is hard,   50
And think of it with pity,
For your great ardour, working through her beauty,
Weighs all too heavily upon my heart.
Love, with your sweetness, make her feel some part
Of the great longing that I have to look
Upon her; do not brook
That with her youth she lead me to the grave:
For she knows not the power she has to please,
Nor how strong is my love,
Nor yet that in her eyes she holds my peace.   60

Your honour will be great for helping thus,
Precious the gift to me;
Because the point is reached where I must see

That I no longer can defend my life:
She who assaults my spirits has such force
That now, unless it be
Your will to spare them, I believe that they
Are brought so low they cannot long survive.
And more, let this fair woman come alive
To your great power that she deserves to feel,   70
For it seems right to grant her all
The retinue of good things upon her way
Since she was born into the world to hold her
Sovereignty and sway
Over the minds of all men who behold her.

[A.M.]

[XXXVIII*]

So deeply do I feel Love's mighty power   1
That I cannot sustain
Much longer all the suffering I lament:
For while his strength increases hour by hour
My own is on the wane
And growing weaker still at every moment.
I say not Love does more than I consent,
For if he did all that my will might bid,
The vital force in me that nature made,
Being finite as it is, could not survive.   10
And here's the very cause of my complaint:
That between power and will there's no accord.
Yet if good will gives birth to some reward,
Then now I ask it, that I may derive
More life from radiant eyes that when they shine
Ever bring comfort to this love of mine.

The rays from those fair eyes enter my own,
My loving eyes, and pour
Their sweetness where my bitterness holds sway;
They know the path, having already gone   20
Along it once before,
And know the place where, through my eyes, that day
They brought Love in and left him there to stay:
Thus, turned on me, those eyes are my reward,
But hidden they bring loss upon the maid
Who owns them, since my loss is such that I
Hold myself dear only to find a way
Of serving her. My thoughts, which Love has made,
See there alone the end they move towards:
An end I crave so strongly that if by   30
Fleeing her I might serve, then willingly
I'd do it, knowing it meant death for me.

54

True love has seized on me, there is no doubt,
Its grasp so firm that I
Would do for it all that I say I will;
Because there is no love as great as that
Which welcomes death in high
And loyal service to another's will.
And in this mind I have been constant still
Since in one moment the resplendent grace   40
That gathers every beauty in her face
Begot the longing that I feel for her.
I am a servant, but when I recall
Of whom, her moods shake not my happiness:
Service refused is service nonetheless;
And if her youth denies me her sweet favour,
I trust the better wisdom time will send,
Provided I survive to see that end.

When I think how, being born of my great love,
Another love reclaims   50
And urges all my powers to working good,
Then my reward seems more than I deserve;
And more, the very name
Of servant in my case is misapplied;
For in those eyes service is a reward
Granted to me by virtue of another.
Yet, since I hold to truth, I must consider
That my desire counts as service too:
In that, although so truly I have tried
To prove myself, not for myself I labour,   60
But for the one who has me in her power,
That glory may be hers from all I do:
I am all hers – an honour, I believe,
That Love has made me worthy to receive.

Love, and no other, could have made me so,
Worthy to be possessed

By one who is not subject to his power,
But coldly stands apart as having no
Care for the loving breast,
Which, without her, cannot endure an hour.   70
For all the many times that I have seen her,
I find fresh beauty still in each new sight;
Therefore in me Love multiplies his might
As much as she is magnified in beauty.
Hence it is only when I am without her
That I remain unmoving in a state
Where Love instructs with suffering and delight,
And both of these together often sting me;
This starts when I lose sight of her, and then
Ends as I find that loveliness again.   80

My lovely song, if you resemble me,
You will not be as proud
As might be justified by so much good:
Therefore, my sweet and loving song, I pray,
Think well, and take the road
With modest bearing and in humble mood.
And if some knight should call you in, take heed;
Before you go with him send out to see
Who are the friends that bear him company,
If you would know what kind of man he is: 90
Because the good dwell ever with the good
(Although an evil man may often be
Found in a fellowship that gives the lie,
Through goodly life, to the foul name he has).
Avoid the wicked both at work and play;
To go with them is never wisdom's way.

My song, seek out, before you go elsewhere,
Our native city's three least vicious men;
Greet the first two of them and, if you can,
Detach the third from friends of evil fame.   100

Tell him no good man on the good makes war
Before he strives to conquer wicked men;
Tell him the man's a fool who will not run
Away from folly for the fear of shame:
In fearing evil there is no dishonour,
And fleeing one brings safety from the other.

[A.M.]

[XXXIX]

Anonymous poet to Dante

Dante Alighieri, praised as having all   I
The wisdom that a body may contain,
A humble friend of yours dared to complain
To his disdainful lady and recall
Your words in his support – to no avail:
For she has struck him with a blade so fine
That by no means can he survive the pain,
Since on his heart the blows already fall.
Therefore revenge on her is yours to take,
For he is conquered; never in her place   10
Shall any woman enter for his sake.
Of all her goodly qualities and grace,
How blithe and young she is, now let me speak,
For Love himself is there, borne in her face.

[A.M.]

[XXXIX a]

Dante to the Anonymous Poet

I, Dante, since to me you make appeal,   1
Now give my answer briefly and in pain,
Without reflection, since I can't sustain
The thought of all the sufferings you feel.
But first one thing I ask you to reveal:
To whom, in citing me, did you complain?
Perhaps a letter sent from me might gain
Admittance there, and every wound would heal.
Yet I believe that if the band* that makes
One know her as unmarried stays in place,   10
She will unsay each cruel word she spoke.
It seems, from all you tell me of her grace,
That she must be as free from sin's sad mark
As any angel high in paradise.

[A.M.]

[XL]

Cino da Pistoia* to Dante

Not long ago Love swore that if I sought 1
To look upon a certain lady, she
Would turn the marvel of her gaze on me,
And by its grace beatify my heart.
Experience teaches me that when Love's dart
Is notched and ready, then he will deny
All promises; so I am loath to die,
Having no skill to play the phoenix part.
Now if I raise my eyes, my heart will crack,
Lose with one blow the little left to live 10
After the other wound that Love once gave.
Dante, what shall I do? For always Love
Invites me on, yet I unmanned hold back,
Fearing the green may prove worse than the black.*

[A.M.]

[X L a]

Dante to Cino

I have once seen a tree without a root,   1
Yet with such vital sap in it that he
Whose son fell in the stream of Lombardy
Drew forth from it new foliage – but no fruit:*
No fruit, indeed, for Nature ruled that out,
Attentive to the tree's deficiency,
And knowing well how false the taste would be,
Since the true nurse was lacking from the start.
A green young girl has thus been known to make
Her entrance through one's gazing eyes to live   10
So deep within that she was loath to leave.
A woman in this colour, I believe,
Is dangerous, and so, for your own sake,
The path to that sweet green you should not take.

[A.M.]

[XLI]

Dante to Cino

Since here nobody cares to speak about   I
The lord to whom both you and I belong,
I seek a way to satisfy the strong
Desire I have to utter such good thought.
For surely there is nothing that you ought
To blame for my dull silence, harsh and long,
Except the place that I am in, where wrong
Is so entrenched that goodness is shut out.*
There is no lady here into whose face
Love comes, and no man ever sighs for love –   10
And he would be a fool who did so here.
Ah, Master Cino, times change for the worse,
Worse for ourselves and for the craft we serve,
Since goodness is received with such scant cheer.

[A.M.]

[XLI a]

Cino to Dante

Where good is heard that here all men forget,   1
Dante, I know not; it has been so long
Since goodness fled away that now the strong
Tempest of evil flashes all about.
Yet to allow the change of time and state
To silence good would put one in the wrong:
You know that God preached clearly to the throng,
And was not silent in the devils' court.
Therefore, if now the world provides no place
To shelter goodness, would you wish to give   10
The homeless cause to suffer even more?
Dear brother, caught in coils of great distress,
By her you love, I pray, cease not to strive
In works, unless your faith has crumbled there.*

[A.M.]

[XLII]

Master Brunetto, here's a fresh young maid*   1
Who comes along to join your Easter feast:
Don't think I mean an Easter when you eat;
She doesn't eat, she's asking to be read.
The means to grasp her meaning are not made
Of hurry, noise or revelling in the street;
You'll need to coax her several times at least
Before she starts to penetrate your head.
And if you find all this is not enough,
You've many Brother Alberts* to explain   10
Even the toughest text that comes to hand.
Join up with them, and promise not to laugh;
And if they find some bits that still aren't plain,
Go and ask Master Giano* in the end.

[A.M.]

[XLIII*]

Now I have reached the point on heaven's wheel*   1
When the horizon, as the sun goes down,
Gives birth to those clear twins* that light the sky,
And when love's star* is far from us and pale
Because the sidelong beam cast by the sun
Bestrides it so and veils it from the eye;
And the cold planet* stands revealed on high
Fully to us in that great arching way
Where each of seven* casts a shorter shade:
And yet I have not laid   10
Aside one single thought of love: it weighs
Upon my mind, that's harder than a stone
In holding fast the image of a stone.

A vagrant wind from Ethiopian sands,
Darkening all the air, arises now,
Moved by the heat that comes from the sun's sphere;
And drives across the sea so dense a band
Of cloud that, if no adverse wind should blow,
It closes in and seals our hemisphere;
And then dissolves, descending on us here   20
In cold white flakes of snow and dismal rain,
So that the very air must weep and mourn:
Yet Love, whose webs are drawn
Aloft whenever the wind mounts again,
Still leaves me not, so fair she is, this lady,
The cruel one, assigned as my liege-lady.

Each bird that follows warmth has flown away,
Leaving the lands of Europe, whose bleak sky
Can never lose the seven freezing stars;*
And others have made truce with tongue to stay   30

65

Silent until the time of green comes by,
Unless the sound be to lament their woes;
And all the animals whose nature shows
In lustiness are now from love untied,
So dampened is their spirit by the cold;
And yet my spirit holds
Ever more love; sweet thoughts are not denied
Or given to me by any change of season,
But by a lady in her youthful season.

The leaves that once the power of the Ram*   40
Drew forth in beauty to adorn the world
Are now long past their term, the grass is dead;
Hidden from us the green of branch or stem,
Except in bay or pine or fir which hold
A foliage evergreen that does not fade;
And so harsh is the season and so hard
It kills the tender flowers the meadows wear
With a sharp frost too piercing to be borne:
And yet Love has not drawn
Out of my heart the thorn he planted there;   50
So I resolve to bear it with me ever,
All my life long, though I should live for ever.

From hidden veins the various springs give vent
To waters that the earth draws up in steam
And vapours from its bowels underground;
So that the path that pleased me when I went
Along it one fine day is now a stream
And will be so till winter's siege is done;
The face of earth resembles polished stone,
And the dead waters harden into glass,   60
Held in a vice by the contracting cold:
Yet in this war I hold
My ground and do not yield a single pace,

Nor will I yield; for if this pain be sweet,
Death must surpass whatever else is sweet.

My song, what will become of me in that
Sweet other season, new and freshly fair,
When love rains from the heavens on earth below,
If here, in frost and snow,
Love is in me alone, and not elsewhere?   70
I shall be like a man that's made of marble,
If this young girl still keeps a heart of marble.

[A.M.]

[XLIV*]

To the short day and the great ring of shade   1
I come, alas, and to the whitening hills
When winter drains the colour from the grass;
Yet my desire does not change its green,
So deep it thrusts its roots in the hard stone
That speaks and hears as if it were a woman.

In the same way this wonder of a woman
Frozen remains like snow that lies in shade;
For she is no more moved than is the stone
By the sweet season that breathes warm on hills,   10
Converting them again from white to green
By covering them with flowers and with grass.

When she puts on a crown woven of grass,
She frees our mind from every other woman;
So well she braids the yellow curls with green
That Love comes there to linger in the shade –
Love that has pent me up in these low hills
More firmly than the mortar binding stone.

More powerful than any precious stone
Her beauty is, and where she wounds no grass   20
Or herb can heal; so that across the hills
And dales I flee, escaping from that woman;
And from her light there's nothing that gives shade,
Not hill, nor wall, nor branches waving green.

I saw her once when she was dressed in green
So that she could have woken in a stone
The selfsame love I bear her very shade;
Then I desired her in a field of grass,

Dreaming her more in love than any woman
Has ever been, encircled by high hills.   30

But rivers shall flow backward to the hills
Before this tender wood, still damp and green,
Catch fire (as love inflames a lovely woman)
For me; and I would choose to sleep on stone
All my life long, and wander, eating grass,
Only to see where her clothes cast a shade.

Whenever the hills cast a blacker shade,
Under her cloak of green will this young woman
Cancel it like a stone beneath the grass.

[A.M.]

[XLV]

You surely see, Love, how this lady   1
Cares nothing for your power at any time,
The power that rules all fair ones as their lady;
And when she knew that she was now my lady,
Perceiving in my face your beam of light,
Of all things cruel she became the lady;
So that her heart seemed not that of a lady,
But of some wild beast who to love is cold;
For in all seasons, whether hot or cold,
She still shows me the likeness of a lady   10
That has been carved out of some lovely stone
By one who knows how best to work in stone.

And I who have more constancy than stone,
Obeying you for beauty of a lady,
Bear secretly the wound made by your stone
When you struck me as if I were a stone
Chafing against your foot too long a time,
A blow that reached my heart where I am stone.
And no one has discovered the rare stone,
By the reflected sun or its own light,   20
Which has within the power enough or light
To guard me from the peril of that stone
So that it may not lead me with its cold
To where in death I shall indeed be cold.

You know, my lord, that with the freezing cold
Water becomes transformed in crystal stone,
There in the north, the home of the great cold,
And into that same element of cold
The air is changed, so water is the lady
Who rules those parts by reason of the cold: 30

In the same way, when I am in her cold
Presence, my blood congeals to ice each time,
And thoughts that will abridge my earthly time
Dissolve into a watery substance cold
That leaves me through those very eyes whose light
Gave entrance once to that relentless light.

She gathers to herself all beauty's light,
And likewise all the cruelties of cold
Run to her heart that lives without your light;
And thus she dazzles me with such a light   40
That I will see her image in a stone
Or anywhere my eyes may cast their light.
From her eyes I receive so sweet a light
That I care not for any other lady:
And would she were more merciful a lady
To me who beg in darkness and in light
Only the place to serve her and the time.
For that alone I wish a longer lifetime.

Therefore, O power existing before time,
Before all motion or corporeal light,   50
Pity me now in my afflicted time;
Enter her heart at last, it is high time,
And find a way to rid it of the cold
That grants me not what others have, my time:
For if you come in your strong stormy time
And find me weakened thus, this noble stone
Will see me lie within a narrow stone,
Never to rise until the end of time,
When I shall see if ever any lady
Was in the world so fair as this fierce lady.   60

Song, in my mind I carry such a lady
Who, though to me she always stays a stone,

Makes me so bold that other men seem stone;
So that I dare to make for one so cold
The newness that in this your form brings light,
A form unthought-of in all earlier time.*

[A.M.]

[XLVI*]

I would be harsh and bitter in my speech   1
As is this stony beauty in her deeds,
In whom each hour breeds
A fiercer nature and a harder mind,
And clothes her with a jasper breastplate which –
Because she either wears it or retreats –
Guards her from any fleet
Shaft that might catch her naked and unbound.
She kills: it will not help to be confined
In compact steel to flee her deadly blows   10
That, winged against her foes,
Shatter all weapons and strike home at will,
So I am saved by neither strength nor skill.

I cannot find a shield she does not break,
Nor any place that from her face might hide me;
As flower on stem, so she
Stands high above and crowns my thought and will.
Of all my suffering no more heed she takes
Than some brave vessel of a waveless sea;
And the weight sinking me   20
Is one that no rhyme can be fit to tell.
Ah, you tormenting and relentless file,
Rasping my life away with stealthy pain,
Why can you not refrain
From gnawing, one by one, my heartstrings through,
As I from telling who gives strength to you?

For when I think of her where others may
Set eyes on me, my heart still trembles, since
I fear that by some glance
All that is in my mind will be betrayed: 30

73

I fear this more than death which eats away,
With the sharp teeth of Love, my every sense;
By anguish so intense
Those senses are consumed, their work delayed.
Love strikes me to the ground, and with the sword
That murdered Dido triumphs over me;*
To him alone my plea
For mercy rises in a humble prayer;
But mercy, Love has vowed, will not be there.

So time and time again he lifts his hand   40
To threaten my frail life, this evil one,
Who holds and pins me down,
Flat on my back and weary of the fight:
Then strident cries mount up within the mind;
And blood that was dispersed through every vein
Turns and flows back again
Towards the summoning heart, and leaves me white.
He strikes below my left arm, so my heart
Is shaken by the sharp rebounding pain:
Then I say: "If again   50
He lifts his hand, Death will have sealed my fate
Even before the blow descends too late."

If only I could see him split the heart
Of that fell woman who quarters mine, I feel
That death would not be all
Darkness – and for her sake I fly to it:
She strikes no less in dark than in the light,
This cutthroat thief who kills or steals man's soul.
Ah, why does she not howl
For me, as I for her, in the hot pit?   60
For at that very moment I would shout
"I'll help you" – and I'd gladly do it there,
And in the flowing hair

That, for my ruin, Love has curled with gold ,
I'd put my hand, and she would like my hold.

If I had those fair tresses in my hand
That have become a lash and scourge for me,
From terce throughout the day
I'd grasp them till the vesper bell had tolled;
And I would not be pitying or kind,   70
Instead I'd act like some rough bear at play,
And take, if love should flay
My back, revenge with blows a thousandfold.
And even more, intense and close, I'd hold
My gaze upon those sparkling eyes that start
A fire in my slain heart;
Thus would I take revenge because she flees;
And then, at last, with love I'd make her peace.

My song, go straight before that woman who
Has pierced my heart and stolen from my breast   80
The thing I craved the most;
Then drive an arrow through her cruel heart:
To take revenge is honour's finest part.

[A.M.]

[XLVII*]

Three women have come to sit around my heart,   1
Around but not within,
For there Love sits alone
And keeps his lordship over my whole life.
So beautiful they are, of worth so great,
That the strong lord – the one
That's in my heart, I mean –
For awe of them can hardly speak himself.
Each seems dismayed and overcome with grief,
Like those who wander weary, chased away,   10
For whom no one will stay,
Whose worth and beauty are of no avail.
According to their tale,
There was a time when they were held most dear:
Now all men hate them, scorning them as vile.
At last they have come here
As to a friendly house, for they know well
That this is where the one I speak of dwells.

One of them breaks into a long lament,
With head on hand that shows   20
Like some sad severed rose;
Her naked arm, supporting sorrow's crown,
Receives the stormy tears her eyes have spent,
Though one hand hides her woes:
Barefoot, ungirt she goes,
Only her bearing shows her high renown.
At first, when through the torn and tattered gown,
He saw those parts that no good man should name,
Love, pitying her shame,
Asked who she was and what had made her rue.   30
"Oh, food of chosen few,"

She answered in a voice where sighs were mixed,
"Kinship is what leads all of us to you:
I, whom grief most afflicts,
Your mother's sister, I am Righteousness;
Poor, as you see, in girdle and in dress."
When she had told him who she was, her story
Brought grief and shame upon
My lord who asked her then
Who came with her, who were the other two.   40
And she, who had been prompt to weep already,
No sooner heard him than
She burned with yet more pain,
Saying: "Can you not grieve when these eyes flow?"
Then she began: "As you must surely know,
The Nile is, at its source, a little stream,
Where the high light supreme
Narrows the shadow of the osier leaves:
Beside the virgin waves
I brought her* forth who now is at my side,   50
Wiping with yellow hair her tears away.
This is my lovely child;
From her own image in the water, she
Brought forth the one* who's further off from me."

Sighs for a moment checked Love's speech with sorrow;
And then, with eyes that first
Were dry but now were moist,
He kindly greeted his afflicted kin.
And then he said, seizing on both his arrows,
"Rise up, be not downcast;   60
These arms I chose as best,
Tarnished, you see, for lack of use, not worn.
Largess and Temperance and others born
Of our own blood are forced to beg their way.
Yet, if this harm be great,

77

Let mankind whom it touches, weep and wail
With eye and tongue, since still
They feel the rays sent by such hostile stars;
Not we of the eternal citadel:
For, wounded though we are,   70
We shall live on, and a new people here
Return to keep this arrow bright and clear."

To me, who hear such noble outcasts take
In words divinely true
Comfort and sorrow too,
Exile becomes an honour that I prize:
For should the force of fate or judgement make
The world transform each new
White flower to a darker hue,
To fall among the good still earns some praise.   80
And were not the fair object of my eyes
Removed by distance from my longing sight
(And this sets me alight),
I'd count as nothing all that weighs upon me.
But now that flame already
Has so far eaten up my flesh and bone
That deep within my breast Death thrusts his key.
Whatever guilt was mine,
Several moons have passed since it was spent,
If guilt expires because a man repents.   90

My song, let no man touch your dress to see
What a fair woman hides from prying eyes:
Let the bare parts suffice;
Deny to everyone the precious fruit
For which all hands reach out.
But should you ever chance to find someone,
A friend to virtue, and he then entreats,
Put fresh new colours on,

Show yourself to him, let that flower prove
How outward loveliness draws hearts in love.   100

My song, go hawk with falcons feathered white,*
My song, go hunting with the sable hounds*
Who forced me to take flight;
They still can grant the peace I seek with them.
They do not, for they know not who I am:
No wise man on forgiveness locks the door,
Forgiveness is high victory in war.

[A.M.]

[XLVIII]

Lord,* if you see these eyes that long to fill   1
With tears for a new heart-destroying grief,
By her* who never leaves you, grant relief,
Remove the cause that keeps them longing still:
With righteous hand repay the man* who kills
Justice, and then seeks refuge with the chief
Tyrant,* from whom he sucks the bane of life,
Flooding the world with venom at his will:
And to your followers' hearts he brings an air
Of such chill fear that all are stricken dumb.   10
But you, love's fire and light of heavenly birth,
Raise up the virtue that lies cold and bare,
Clothed in your spotless veil now let her come:
Without her, there can be no peace on earth.

[A.M.]

[XLIX*]

Grief sends into my heart a bold desire,   1
A friend to truth, and eager to be heard;
So, ladies, if my words
Berate the sins of almost everyone,
Marvel not, but confess
How vile and base your own desires are:
For Love allowed your beauty to be born
For virtue; this alone
Was beauty's end when the decree was made
That now you sin against.   10
I say to those of you by love possessed:
If virtue should be ours
And beauty ever yours,
And if to make two one be in Love's power,
Then you should love no longer,
But rather veil the beauty you were given,
Since virtue's gone that once was beauty's aim.
Alas, what must I say?
I say what fine disdain,
How laudable it would be in a woman   20
To say farewell to her own beauty's burden.

Men turn their back on virtue and forsake her:
Not men, but evil beasts in human dress.
O God, that man should thus
Abase himself from master into slave –
Indeed, from life to death!
Virtue, as always subject to her maker,
Obeys him, brings him honour, so that Love,
In his blest court above,
Appoints her to his council in a place   30
With those of greatest worth:

And from her lady's lovely gates goes forth
In joy and then returns;
With joy where she sojourns
She proves herself in service loyally;
On her brief journey she
Preserves, adorns, increases all she finds;
Death cannot touch her for she takes no heed.
O handmaid, pure indeed,
With heaven's measure at need;   40
You alone give true lordship and are signed
As the unfailing treasure of mankind.

The slave of a base slave, not of a lord,
Is what someone becomes who goes astray
From such a handmaid's way.
Count up the double loss* and you will find
The cost of parting from her:
This slavish lord is so possessed by pride
That those clear inward eyes that light the mind
Are closed and leave him blind;   50
So that we wander after one whose gaze
Is fixed on foolish matter.
But that these words of mine may serve you better,
From whole I turn to part
And use a simpler art,
So it should be less hard to grasp my speech;
For dark words rarely reach
The intellect that's covered by a veil;*
Thus one who speaks with you should make things plain:
But this I urge again   60
(For your sake, not for mine):
Despise all men, their pleasures scorn as vile;
Shared joys reveal a mind that's shared as well.

A man enslaved is one who follows close
Behind his lord, along a painful road,
Not knowing where it leads;
Or like a miser following wealth which is
The whole world's only master.
The miser runs, but runs away from peace:
O thought made blind by foolish will, for his   70
Mad quest sees not how this
Great sum that he keeps striving to exceed
Recedes from him for ever!
But look, here comes the last great leveller:
Tell me, what have you done,
Poor miser, blind, undone?
You answer "Nothing" – what else can you say?
Cursed be the cradle where you lay
For flattering so many dreams in vain!
Cursed be your daily bread; if it were cast   80
To dogs there'd be less waste!
For your whole day is passed
Grasping and clasping with both hands the gain
That then so quickly slips away again.

Men know no measure in amassing wealth,
No measure when they hoard the wealth they own:
Many by this alone
Are driven to bondage, nor can one prevent
That doom without a fight.
Fierce Fortune, are you there? Where are you, Death,   90
That you do not share out what's left unspent?
But whom you should content
I cannot say, for heaven has laid down
Strict limits to our light.*
Reason's to blame that has not put this right;
And if he pleads "But I'm not free",
That poor defence is fit to be

Made by a lord who's mastered by a slave!
This shame is doubly grave,
For if you look where I point out you should –   100
False animals, self-made, who bring such ill
On others and yourselves as well –
You see men lost in marsh and hill:
These men, before whose virtue vice has fled,
Go naked while you clothe yourselves in mud.

Virtue, who calls her enemies to make peace,
Comes forth and, standing in the miser's sight,
Flourishes something bright,
Hoping to tempt him to her; but in vain,
For he evades the snare.*   110
She circles round him, calling without cease,
So eager that she throws the morsel down;
But he will not be drawn:
And if, when she has left, he takes the bait,
It seems that all his care
Is what the gift will cost him, so that there
No praise can come his way.
Hear what I have to say:
Delays or sullen looks or vanity
Undo all charity*   120
And turn the gift into a sale; the buyer
Alone can tell you how it costs him dear.
You truly want to hear?
The wound is so severe
That from then on refusal won't seem bitter.
The miser thus ruins himself and others.

Ladies, I have unveiled, at least in part,
The baseness of those men who gaze on you,
So you may scorn that crew:
Though there is much more ugliness concealed   130

That is not fit to speak.
Each one assembles every vice, and that
Confounds all mutual friendship in the world:
For love's leaves are unfurled
When a good root's informed by good anew,
As like appeals to like.
See, ladies, the conclusion that I make:
A woman who sees good
In her own beauty should
Never believe the love of such vile men;   140
If you believe it, then
Count beauty evil, love a word we know
And use to name a bestial appetite!
Perish that lady's light
Who thinks her beauty might
Be severed from her natural goodness so –
As if in reason's plot no love could grow!

My song, there is a lady from our land
Dwelling not far from here;
Courteous, wise and fair   150
Men call her, and know not they mean the same
Each time they say her name,
Bianca or Giovanna or Countess:*
Go to her now with mien discreet and plain;
At first with her remain
So that you may explain
Both who you are and also why I sent you;
Then go upon your way as she directs you.

[A.M.]

[L]

Cino da Pistoia to Dante

Dante, when by some chance the longing love   1
Abandons hope as unfulfilled and vain –
Hope planted in the mind as beauty's grain
And that the eyes have caused to grow and live –
I say, if death* should grant the soul reprieve,
And Love, rather than two extremes,* still reign;
Then, with no more to fear and quite alone,
That soul is free to find another love.
She who is mistress of all things leads me
To say this, since, alas, Love once again   10
Enters me through the window of the eye.
Before I'm killed by black and white,* explain,
You, who have been both in and out* already,
How true or false is this belief of mine.

[A.M.]

[L a]

Dante to Cino

Indeed, I have kept company with Love   1
Since my ninth revolution of the sun,*
And I know how he uses spur and rein
And how beneath him one may groan and laugh.
Reason and virtue urged against him prove
No better than a bell men ring to drown
The sound of tempest, thinking to calm down
The war of clouds that thunders high above.
Thus in the round arena that contains
Love's combats no free will was ever free,   10
So that good counsel shoots its darts in vain.
Love may well use new spurs; whatever be
The pleasure that now freshly leads us on,
Follow we must if the old one be weary.

[A.M.]

[LI]

*Cino da Pistoia to Marchese Moroello Malaspina**

As I was searching for the ore that hides   I
*The perfect gold that awes each noble mind,**
An evil thorn, Marchese, chanced to wound*
My heart so that I die from loss of blood.
Not for the end of natural life I shed
These tears, but more for what I do not find:
My fate by such a planet is defined
That where I lose I willingly abide.
And there are further pains I could recount,
But that I think the tale of them would offer   10
*You too much pleasure in what makes me suffer.**
Yet still, before I come to die, my master
*May well transform to gold the rugged mount,**
*Who from cold marble once brought forth a fount.**

[A.M.]

88

[L I a]

Dante to Cino on behalf of Moroello Malaspina

That clear sweet voice of yours has surely made   1
You worthy to find treasure, but your sound
And fickle heart that never felt Love's wound
Misleads you so that you have always strayed.
Through every pore I feel the thorn invade,
Leaving the hurt that sighs alone can tend,
Yet I have found the precious ore refined
Into the power that my pallor displays.
It's not the sun's fault if a blind face can't
See when he sets and rises, it is rather   10
The cruel sad condition such men suffer.
And even if I saw you weep a shower
To prove that your fine words were truly meant,
I'd still be far from trusting your intent.

[A.M.]

[LII]

Dante to Cino

Cino, I truly thought that nevermore   1
Would I take up this poetry of ours,
For now my ship must hold another course,
Being, as it is, much farther from the shore.
But since it seems that any hook can draw
You back again, according to the voice
That I keep hearing, I've resolved to force
My tired fingers to the pen once more.
A man who falls in love the way you do,
Now here, now there, now chained and then unbound, 10
Shows that Love's wound for him is but a scratch.
So, if the heart thus lightly whirls you round,
With virtue mend that fault, I beg of you,
Making your deeds agree with your sweet speech.

[A.M.]

[LIIa]

Cino to Dante

Dante, now ever since a bitter law   I
Exiled me from my native land,* my course
Takes me from where the Infinite Beauty's force
Showed the best beauty she could ever draw.
I have gone weeping through the world, a poor
Wretch death disdains; yet when some beauty shares
A likeness with that first, my heart declares
That this one makes the wound that I deplore.
Nor have I ever yet escaped the reach
Of those first pitiless arms, for I have found   10
No help except what fixed despair can do:
For always the same beauty holds me bound,
And I must take delight if any such
Beauty appears in other women too.

[A.M.]

[LIII*]

Love, since I have no choice but to complain   1
So that I may be heard
And show to men how all my strength is spent,
Grant me the will and mastery so to mourn
That my unfettered words
Speak feelingly of what I must lament.
You wish my death, and I am well content:
But who'll excuse me if I cannot tell
What you have made me feel?
Who will believe in my captivity?   10
Yet if you give me speech to match my torment,
Ensure, my lord, that this cruel woman will
Wait till I die before she hears the tale:
For if she knew the things I hear within me,
Her lovely face would be defaced with pity.

She comes unchecked to my imagination;
I can no more stop this
Than I can can block the thought that brings her there.
My rash soul, working to its own destruction,
Depicts her as she is,   20
Shapes its own pain, this image fierce and fair:
Gazing its fill until it cannot bear
The unsated longing that her eyes incite,
The burning soul ignites
With anger at itself who lit the fire.
What argument can reason offer where
This sudden tempest rages round about?
Anguish, which cannot be contained, breathes out
Sighs through the mouth and forces men to hear,
And also gives the eyes their meed of tears.   30

The hostile image does not change, being so
Victorious and cruel
That the will cedes to her dominion:
In love with her own self, she makes me go
To where she truly dwells,*
Like following like, as it has always done.
I see that I am snow that seeks the sun,
But have no choice. Under another's sway
A man makes his own way,
On his own feet, to where the scaffold waits;   40
And I, when near her, seem to hear someone
Saying, "Come quick and see this fellow die!"
I turn to see if any standing by
Can help me, and am struck with sudden light
From eyes that slay me, though they have no right.

What I become thus stricken, Love, you tell,
Not I, for you remain
To see me lifeless; and although the soul
Regains the heart after a time, yet still
Unknowing and oblivion   50
Have been with it throughout the interval.
When I arise and gaze upon the cruel
Wound that undid me when I felt the stroke,
There is no comfort I can take
To stop myself from trembling with fear.
And then my face, drained of all colour, will
Show what the lightning striking me was like;
For though the flash came from a smiling look,
My face remains long after darkened there,
Because the spirit is not free from care.   60

Here, in a mountain valley, Love, you have
Brought me to such a state,
And by this stream I always feel your strength:

93

You knead me at your will, dead or alive,
Thanks to the cruel light
That with its flashes shows the way to death.
I see no ladies here, no men of worth
And feeling mind, alas, to hear my grief:
Thus I find no relief
From others if this woman care not for me.   70
This outlaw from your court,* my lord, goes forth,
Heedless of all the arrows in your sheaf:
She makes her pride a breastplate of such proof
That every shaft is blunted, biting vainly
On armour while her heart remains in safety.

Go on your way, my little mountain song:
Perhaps you will see Florence, my own city,
That still, stripped bare of pity
And void of love, shuts me outside her bounds;
If you should enter there, tell them: "No longer   80
Can he who made me be your enemy:
I come here from a place where he is bound by
Such chains that even if your harshness turned
To grace he has no freedom to return."

[A.M.]

[LIV]

Along that road where beauty makes her way   1
To rouse Love who lies sleeping in the mind,
Lisetta passes all-too boldly, and
Is confident that she can capture me.
She comes to take her stand under that tower
Which opens only when the soul agrees,
But suddenly she hears a voice which says:
"Turn back! There is no point in waiting here:
There is another lady on the throne,
Already here with Love inside this house: 10
She asked, he gave, the rod when she first came."
Lisetta sees that she will never reign
Where Love is living and, sent packing thus,
She has to turn away, covered in shame.

[J.G.N.]

FROM
Vita Nuova

[III]

For every gentle heart* and captive soul
To whom this verse arrives, in hope that they
Will write back and expound its sense to me,
These greetings in the name of Love, their lord.
The night already had traversed a third
Of those set hours when stars light up the sky
When Love appeared before me suddenly,
And in a form I shudder to recall.
Love first seemed full of joy, and in his hand
He held my heart, while in his arms he had   10
My lady shrouded in a cloth, asleep.
He woke her then, and with my heart that burned
Devoutly fed her, though she was afraid:
At last I saw him take his leave and weep.

[A.M.]

[VII]

O all of you who pass* along Love's way,
Pause here, take heed, and say
If there was ever grief as great as mine;
With patience simply hear me out, I pray,
Think to yourselves how I
Am now the house and key of every pain.
Not my small worth, but Love's nobility
Once granted me the free
Gift of a life so sweet and so serene
That often at my back I heard men say: 10
"How then, by Heaven, has he
Deserved a heart so light? What has he done?"
Now I have lost the blithe exultant mood
That came to me from Love's own precious store,
And I am left so poor
That now I hardly dare to write a word.
Therefore I choose to act like those who bear
Some loss that shame has made them wish to hide;
The joy I show outside
Conceals a heart that wastes away in tears.   20

[A.M.]

[VIII]

Weep, lovers,* since you see that Love now weeps,
And hear the reason why his tears awake;
Love hears the crying that these ladies make
To Pity, as their eyes show forth their grief.
For churlish Death has worked its ruin deep
Within a gentle heart, from which it takes
All graces that, as well as honour, make
A woman worthy to be praised on earth.
Hear how Love chose to honour her, for there
I saw him mourning in his own true form   10
Over the lovely image without life;
And often he would look to heaven above,
Where that sweet soul had gone to find its home,
Who was a lady once so blithe and fair.

[A.M.]

[VIII]

Death, churlish villain,* ever pity's foe,
Ancient mother of woe,
Onerous sentence incontestable,
Since you have given the heart such cause to dwell
In heavy thoughts, I still
Tire my weary tongue by railing so.
But if I truly wish that you should grow
Detested, I must show
Your evil guilt as guilty of all ill –
Not that your crime is hidden, but to fill   10
With greater anger all
Who draw from love the nurture that they know.
You have bereft the world of courtesy
And that which in a woman merits praise;
It is the loving grace
And life of joyful youth that you destroy.
No more will I reveal who she may be
Than from her noted qualities we learn.
No one who cannot earn
Salvation may expect her company.   20

[A.M.]

[IX]

Riding along* and brooding on the road
That I was loath to take, the other day,
I met Love in the middle of the way,
Advancing like a traveller meanly clad.
He seemed to me downcast as if he had
Lost much of his habitual lordly sway;
Sighing he came and, since he would not stay
To look on other men, he bowed his head.
He saw me, called my name, and said: "I now
Come from a distant region where your heart   10
Once chose to dwell because I willed it thus:
I bring it back to serve new loveliness."
And then he vanished as so large a part
Of him passed into me – I knew not how.

[A.M.]

[XII]

Ballad, I pray you,* seek out Love and bring
Him with you to my lady, so that there,
When you have offered my excuse to her,
My lord may then expound what you have sung.

Your bearing is so courteous that you could
Go anywhere you like
Boldly, without an escort, and not fear;
And yet to take Love with you might be good,
Ballad, for safety's sake;
To go without him would be far from sure.   10
For I believe the lady who should hear
The cause you plead is so displeased with me
That if you come without Love's company,
Her scornful greeting may dishonour you.

When you are there with Love, let sweetest sounds
Accompany these words
(After imploring mercy of her grace):
"My lady, if it please you, he who sends
Me thus begs to be heard
Through me, if he has any true excuse.   20
Love comes with me, Love who delights to use
Your beauty to make him change countenance:
Judge for yourself why Love has turned his glance
Towards another, since his heart's unchanged."

Tell her: "My lady, this man's heart has stayed
Constant, with steadfast will,
And every thought intent on serving you:
Yours from the first, and he has never strayed."
Then, if she doubts you still,

Let her ask Love who knows that this is true.   30
And, at the last, I bid you, humbly sue
That if she has no mind to pardon me,
She may command my death, and she shall see
A servant who well knows how to obey.

   Before you take your leave of her, tell Love,
Who is compassion's key
And has the skill to further my good cause:
"Thanks to the force this melody can give,
Stay with her and be free
To speak about your servant at your ease;   40
And if she grants forgiveness through your pleas,
See that her gracious smiling brings the news."

   Sweet ballad, when you go to meet her, choose
A time when she will greet and honour you.

[A.M.]

[XIII]

My thoughts all speak of love, and they display
Among themselves such great diversity
That while one makes me wish his mastery,
Another holds that madness lies that way;
Another comes with hope that brings me joy,
Another has me weeping frequently:
Only in begging pity all agree,
With fearful heart that trembles as they pray.
Therefore, I do not know which theme to choose,
Eager to write – of what I do not know,   10
Lost in love's labyrinth and wandering still.
And if I seek to reconcile them all,
I needs must call, at last, upon my foe,
My lady Pity,* to defend my cause.

[A.M.]

[XIV]

When other ladies mock me,* you no less
Laugh at my looks, and do not call to mind
What makes me look so strangely when I bend
My gazing eyes upon your loveliness.
If you but knew the cause, Pity would cease
Her old hard ways towards me and be kind,
For Love gains such assurance when he finds
Me close to you that boldly he will press
Among my fearful spirits and strike them down;
For some he kills and others he drives out,   10
Till he alone remains to look on you.
This makes me seem another, yet I do
Not change so much as not to hear the shouts
Of banished spirits howling in their pain.

[A.M.]

[XV]

All that I meet with in the memory dies
When I resolve to see you, fair delight;
But in your presence I hear Love who says:
"If death is fearsome to you, now take flight."
The fainting pallor of my face betrays
The swooning heart that gropes for some support;
And, in the dizzying tremors that arise,
"Die! Die!" the very stones seem to cry out.
He sins who sees me in this state and fails
To comfort my bewildered soul, at least   10
By showing the compassion which comes forth
From the same pity that your mockery kills –
A pity roused by these dead eyes that cast
A spent regard that only looks for death.

[A.M.]

[XVI]

The memory recalls time and again
The dark conditions Love confers on me,
Until self-pity drives me to complain:
"Alas, who else endures such misery?"
For Love assails me with such sudden pain
That life almost forsakes me, though one true
And living spirit survives, who still remains
Only because he always speaks of you.
At this I brace myself to act and rise,
Pallid and void of strength, to make my way   10
To look upon you, thinking to be cured;
And yet no sooner do I lift my eyes
Than tremors shake the heart and chase away
The feeble soul pulsating in my blood.

[A.M.]

[XIX]

Ladies that have intelligence of love,*
I tell you of my lady, not because
I think to do her justice with my praise,
But to relieve the burden on my mind.
When I consider her great worth, Love leaves
So sweet a feeling in me that my voice
(But that I then lose courage) might arouse
By speech alone such love in all mankind.
I will not look for the exalted kind
Of speech that makes me shrink away in fear,   10
But I will tell of all that makes her dear
In words too light for her, and yet designed
For loving ladies and for maidens too,
Not to be heard by anyone but you.*

In the eternal mind an angel cries,
Saying: "We see, Lord, how the low world breeds
A miracle incarnate that proceeds
From a soul shining even to this height."
And heaven, where no imperfection lies,
Save lack of her, begs that the Lord concede   20
Her advent for which saints in glory plead.
Pity alone remains to take our part,*
For God, who has my lady in His thought,
Proclaims: "Have patience, loved ones: while I please,
Your hope will linger where one man foresees
That he will lose her. It shall be his fate
To say in hell: 'O you, born to be lost,
I have beheld the hope of all the blessed.'"*

My lady is desired in heaven above:
Now I would show her excellence and declare   30

That ladies who are eager to appear
Noble themselves should keep her company.
For, where she walks, a chill is cast by Love
On evil hearts to freeze the thoughts they bear.
Yet if such men could stand to look on her,
They would turn noble, or else cease to be.
If she finds someone who deserves to see
Her as she is, then he will prove the whole
Power her presence has to save the soul,
Humbled, forgetting every injury.   40
She has one greater grace that God has sent:
No one she speaks with makes an evil end.

   Love says of her: "How can a mortal be
So beautiful a creature and so pure?"
And looking yet again, thinks he would swear
God made her with a miracle in mind.
Her hue is pearl-like, and its quality
Does not exceed what makes a woman fair:
What goodness Nature bears was born in her;
By her example beauty is defined.   50
Her eyes, wherever she may turn them, send
Forth in a flame spirits of love that strike
The eyes of anyone who meets her look
And then pass through to where the heart is found.
You will see Love depicted in her face;
But that is where no man can fix his gaze.

   My song, when I have sent you forth, I know
That you will speak with ladies on your way.
Now, therefore, since I brought you up to be
Like Love's own humble daughter, young and plain,*   60
I bid you ask, wherever you may go:
"Sent as I am for this, teach me, I pray
The path to her whose praises I display."

And, that your journey should not be in vain,
Do everything you can not to remain
Among low-minded people, but confide
In women or some courteous man to guide
You quickly to the end you should attain.
You will find Love together with her there;
So, as you should, commend me to his care.   70

[A.M.]

[XX]

Love and the noble heart* are ever one,
Just as the wise man, in his verses, said;
One has such being when the other's gone
As has the rational soul when reason's fled.
Nature in love creates them – Love to own
The heart as mansion where he is the lord;
And deep within those chambers he sleeps on*
For short or longer seasons undisturbed.
Then beauty comes: some virtuous woman's look
Pleases the eye so much that in the heart   10
Desire for the pleasing thing is born,
And sometimes dwells there long enough to wake
The spirit of love – which is the same effect
Roused in a woman by a worthy man.

[A.M.]

[XXI]

My lady's eyes bear Love, and thus impart
Nobility to what she looks upon;*
All turn to see her passing, and the man
She greets endures such trembling of the heart
That, pallid and with downcast eyes, he starts
To sigh for all his failings; pride is gone
And wrath must flee her presence. Ladies, then,
Help me to pay her homage with my art.
All gentleness and every thought that's humble
Come to the hearts of those who hear her voice,   10
So that the one who sees her first is praised.
And, at her slightest smile, the vision raised
Is more than mind can hold or words express,
She is so rare a wonder and so gentle.

[A.M.]

[XXII]

You ladies who proceed* with eyes cast down,
Soberly bearing all the signs of woe,
Where have you come from, for your aspect now
Seems more like pity's image than your own?
Is it our gentle lady you have seen,
Love in her face, bathed with the tears that flow?
Speak, ladies, for my heart has told me so,
Seeing you pass with grave and noble mien.
And if you come from such a grief as this,
I beg you, stay a little while with me,   10
And do not hide the truth of how she is.
Your eyes are sore with weeping, and to see
You thus disfigured is enough to cause
The fear that shakes my heart so violently.

[A.M.]

[XXII]

Can you be he who spoke to us alone
Those verses written in our lady's praise?
It is his voice that echoes in our ears,
And yet in looks you seem another man.
Why do you weep so sorely that you win
Pity indeed from everyone that hears?
Were you yourself there to behold her tears,
That now you cannot hide the grief within?
Leave weeping then to us, whose steps are sad
(All comfort here would be a sin), for we   10
Have heard her speaking through the tears she shed.
The suffering in her face is plain to see,
So that no one could look and long abide
That gaze, but must fall weeping there and die.

[A.M.]

[XXIII]

A lady moved by pity,* young in years,
Graced with all gentleness, was by my side
While I was calling Death to come to me;
And seeing how my eyes were full of tears,
And listening to the wild words that I cried,
She also wept for fear most bitterly.
And by the clamour of that weeping she
Drew other women near to where I lay,
Who then sent her away
And gathered round me, seeking to restore   10
My senses. "Sleep no more,"
One said; and yet another: "Tell us why
Are you in such distress?" And then I came
Out of my dream, calling my lady's name.

Such was the sorrow that suppressed my voice,
So broken was my speech with grief, that I
Alone, within my heart, could hear that name.
But Love insisted that I turn my face
Towards those women who were standing by,
Though it was wholly overcome by shame.   20
Into my spent regard a colour came
That made them speak of death: I heard one say:
"Ah, comfort him, I pray,"
Echoed by others in a hushed refrain;
And over and again:
"What drained you of your strength? What sight? What dream?"
Somewhat restored at last, with courage new,
I said: "Now I shall tell it all to you.

"As I considered how my life is frail,
How fragile and impermanent its stay,   30

117

Love in my heart began to weep and cry;
At which so lost in anguish was my soul
That I was moved, in sighing thought, to say:
'Surely, in time, my lady too must die.'
Then such distress laid hold of me that my
Dejected eyelids closed, weighed down by care,
And so enfeebled were
My spirits that each wandered off alone;
And I, to visions prone
And far from truth and knowledge, seemed to see   40
Faces of women, glaring angrily,
And still repeating: 'You will die, will die.'

   "In that deceptive dream I came to where
I saw strange things and found myself alone
Lost in some doubtful place I did not know:
And women passed me with dishevelled hair,
Some weeping, others heaving sighs and groans
That seemed like fiery arrows winged with woe;
I saw the sun grow dark and, stealing slow,
The stars emerge in heaven, one by one,   50
All weeping with the sun;
Birds in their flight fell lifeless from the air,
And the earth shook for fear;*
Then came a pale weak man, who in a low
Faint voice said to me: 'What! Have you not heard?
Your lady, once so beautiful, is dead.'

   "I raised my eyes, already wet with tears,
And saw what seemed to be a rain of manna,
Angels returning to their heavenly home,
With a small cloud before them in the air,   60
Which they all followed, crying out 'Hosanna!'*
Had they used other words, then I would give them.
Then Love said: 'I shall not conceal it; come
With me to see our lady where she lies.'

So my false fantasies*
Took me away to see my lady dead;
There I saw women spread
A veil to cover her; yet in that form
Such true humility had found a place
One would have thought she said: 'I am at peace.'   70

   "Taught by my sorrow, I became so humble,
Seeing humility given form in her,
That I said: 'Death, you are most dear to me;
For surely you have also been made noble
By being with my lady, as you were:
You must show mercy, harsh you cannot be.
I am so eager to be yours, you see,
That now I bear your image: come into
This heart that calls on you.'
Then I departed, mourning rites all done;   80
And when I was alone
I said, with eyes raised to the realm on high:
'Blessèd is he who looks on you, fair soul!'
Then you, in mercy, woke me with your call."

[A.M.]

[XXIV]

Within my heart* I felt a spirit of love,
Who had been sleeping, suddenly awake;
And then I saw Love coming from far off,
But hardly knew him for that joyful look;
And he said: "Now, indeed, be sure to give
Me honour," smiling with each word he spoke.
After a while, I turned to see where Love
Had come from, and beheld, as I looked back,
Both ladies, Vanna and Bice, drawing near
To where I was, so that one marvel came   10
Behind another. Now my memory
Tells me Love said: "The first who passes here
Is Primavera, and the other's name
Is Love, because she looks so much like me."*

[A.M.]

[XXVI]

With such a gentle,* such a noble air
My lady gives her greeting that speech dies
On every trembling tongue, and no man's eyes
Are ever bold enough to look on her.
Clothed in humility, she passes there,
Still gracious amid all the praise she hears;
As if come down from heaven, she appears
To be a miracle manifested here.
Her beauty, as it strikes the gazing eye,
Dispatches such a sweetness to the heart   10
That only those who feel it understand.
And swiftly from her lips she seems to send
A tender loving spirit who finds out
The yearning soul and stays to whisper: "Sigh."

[A.M.]

[XXVI]

He sees all goodness perfectly who sees
My lady among ladies; surely they
Who go with her should give God thanks for this
Resplendent grace that He has sent their way.
There is such power in her loveliness
That it awakes no envy, but its sway
Makes others walk with her, clothed in the dress
Of gentleness and love and constant faith.
To see her renders every creature humble:
Not only is she fair herself, but all   10
Women receive new honour through her praise.
And in her bearing she appears so noble
That it is something no one can recall
Without love's sweetness breaking forth in sighs.

[A.M.]

[XXVII]

So long has Love been lord* of me and taught
Me how to live according to his law,
That just as he was harsh to me before,
So now he gently dwells within my heart.
Thus it is when he makes my strength depart
And all my spirits run away in fear
That in my fragile soul I know such store
Of sweetness that my face turns pale with it.
Love has such power that he gives a voice
To spirits as they move, and out they come,   10
Calling my lady's name
And begging her to grant me yet more bliss.
This happens every time she looks at me –
Such sweetness no man thought could ever be.

[A.M.]

[XXXI]

These eyes that see the heart* in pain and grieve
Are so afflicted by the tears they shed
That now they are exhausted and run dry.
Thus, if I seek some other way to give
Vent to the grief that draws me on to death,
It is in words that I must learn to sigh.
Since, gentle ladies, I recall how I
Was glad to speak, when she was yet alive,
About my lady openly with you,
So here my speech is to   10
None but such gentle hearts as women have;
And I shall tell of her with tears, for now
She has gone up to heaven suddenly,
And left Love here below to mourn with me.

Now Beatrice has gone to heaven on high,
The blessèd kingdom where she shares the peace
Of angels, and has left you here forlorn:
She was not rapt from us like others by
Excess of cold or heat,* but by the grace
Of her surpassing goodness, that alone: 20
For out of her humility there shone
A light that pierced the heavens with such strength
That the Eternal marvelled at the glow
And felt sweet longing grow
To call such dear perfection to Himself.
And thus He made her rise from here below
Because He saw this wretched life to be
Unworthy of her high nobility.

From that fair body now the noble soul
Has risen up to glory, full of grace,*   30

124

And finds a dwelling that is fit for her.
The man who speaks of this and does not fall
To weeping has a stony heart so base
That no kind spirit ever enters there.
No heart that's vile and mean can ever bear
A mind so high that it can form or know
Some image of her; thus it does not weep:
But to all those who keep
The memory of what she was, and how
Death ravished her from us, there comes a deep   40
Sorrow that longs to sigh and die of grief,
And so their souls are stripped of all relief.

   Anguish invades with every sighing breath
When thought that weighs on the dejected mind
Recalls to me the one who cleft my heart:
And very often, as I think on death,
It breeds in me such longing that I find
My cheeks grow pale to sense how life departs.
And when imagination plays its part,
Intent on her, such torment comes to me   50
From every side that I awake in pain;
And I become as one
Cut off by shame from all men's company.
Then weeping in my lonely sad refrain,
I call to Beatrice: "Are you now dead?"
And as I call her, I am comforted.

   Sorrowing tears and sighs of deep distress
Consume my lonely heart, but anyone
Who heard me would feel pity for my grief;
Nor is there any tongue that can express   60
How I have lived on earth since she has gone
Above and passed into the other life:
And therefore, gentle ladies, even if

I wished, I still could not describe my state,
So bitter is the life I undergo;
And I am brought so low
That all men say: "We leave you to your fate,"
Seeing the mortal pallor of my brow.
But yet my lady sees what I endure,
And I still hope for my reward from her.   70

   Go weeping now from me, my piteous song,
Until you meet those ladies and sweet maids
To whom your sisters made*
Their music once and brought the news of joy:
And, as the child of sorrow, take your way
Disconsolate to them, and there abide.

   [A.M.]

[XXXII]

Come, O you gentle hearts,* to hear my sighs,
Since Pity has desired you should do so,
For they arise disconsolate and go;
Yet were it not for sighing, I should die.
For if I could not sigh, why then my grief
Would all too often need my eyes to flow
With compensating tears, and that is how
My heart that mourns her loss would find relief.
Time after time, those sighs will call upon
My noble lady who has gone to where   10
She finds a world more fit for her than this;
And sometimes you will hear how they deplore
This wretched life, voicing the pain of one
Whose soul is sad, forsaken by its bliss.

[A.M.]

[XXXIII]

When I recall, alas, that nevermore
Shall I again behold
The lady who has brought such pain to me,
The memory gathers to my heart such sore
Affliction that I cry:
"Why do you not depart from me, my soul?
You are already weary of the world,
And now the greater torments that will weigh
Upon you fill my prescient mind with fear."
Thus I call Death, my dear   10
Soothing and sweet repose; to him I say:
"Come here to me," with so much love that I
Am racked with envy of all those who die.

My sighs come crowding forth as if to blend
Into one cry of pity
That calls aloud on Death and will not cease;
Since it was to his mercy that I turned
My longing and my pleas
When his grim power seized upon my lady;
For then the perfect grace that was her beauty   20
Became transformed, withdrawing from our sight,
A beauty of the spirit, so refined
That high in heaven it shines
With beams of love to give the angels light –
Those subtle intellects amazed to see
The splendour of such great nobility.*

[A.M.]

128

[X X X I V]

First Beginning

Into my mind there came* the gentle lady
Who, for her worth and merit, the Most High
Placed in that heaven of humility
Where she now shares the dwelling place of Mary.

Second Beginning

Into my mind there came the gentle one
Whom Love now mourns; and in that moment you
Were drawn by her great worth to come and view
The piece I happened to be working on.
Love, sensing her within my mind again,
Had woken in my shattered heart, and to
My sighs he said, "Go forth," and so they do,
Taking their leave to go their way in pain.
They left my breast, lamenting with a sound
So plaintive that it often makes my eyes   10
Wet with the tears that cannot help but flow.
But those who went most painfully were the sighs
Who said: "It was this day, O noble mind,
That you rose up to heaven a year ago."

[A.M.]

[XXXV]

With my own eyes* I saw how pity came
Into your face when you beheld the way
I look and bear myself distractedly,
Lost in my sorrow, as I often am.
I knew that you were thinking of the lame
Obscure existence that my looks display;
So fear possessed my heart lest I betray
My state with tears and thus increase my shame.
Therefore I took my leave, feeling how near
I was to weeping then, for at the sight   10
Of you that day my grieving heart was stirred.
And after, in my sorrowful soul, I said:
"Love dwells with her, and he is surely that
Same Love that sends me on my way in tears."

[A.M.]

[XXXVI]

No woman's countenance has ever borne
Love's pallor and its pity at the sight
Of one whose weeping eyes reveal his plight
With such a wondrous grace as you have shown
In your sad colour when you see my own
Dejected face before you. So the thought
Of you recalls something that brings a great
Fear that my shattered heart will break again.
I cannot check my ravaged eyes that set
Their hopes on seeing you, time after time,   10
With such a will to weep as now is theirs:
And you increase the fires that consume
Those eyes that seek the sight of you; and yet
Once in your presence they can find no tears.

[A.M.]

[XXXVII]

"The bitter tears, O eyes, that you once let
Fall in your grief for such a weary while,
Have prompted others to shed tears as well,
As you have seen, in pity for your state.
But now it seems that you would soon forget
To weep, if I should be forsworn and fail
To contradict all reasons for that fall,
Reminding you of her for whom you wept.
Your fickle mood weighs heavy in my thought
And terrifies me, for I greatly dread   10
One woman and the power of her eyes.
Except in death, you never should forget
Your gracious lady who herself is dead."
Thus says my heart within, and then it sighs.

[A.M.]

[XXXVIII]

There is a gentle thought that comes to sit
And speak of you, and often dwells with me,
Discoursing there of love so tenderly
That soon the listening heart consents to it.
"Now who is this", the soul asks of the heart,
"That comes to soothe the mind, and how can he
Thus work upon us with a mastery
That leaves no room for any other thought?"
The heart replies: "O pensive soul, this is
A wondrous spirit newly born of love,   10
Who brings his own desires here before me;
His very life and all his powers derive
Only from her compassionate eyes who was
So deeply moved to see our misery."

[A.M.]

[XXXIX]

Alas, the force of many sighs that come
From thoughts within the heart where they were born
Has left my eyes no power to return
The gaze of anyone who looks at them;
And they are so outworn that now they seem
Two orbs whose sole desire is to mourn,
And shed such tears that they have often been
Encircled with Love's crown of martyrdom.
These thoughts, these sighs that I breathe out become
So fraught with anguish in the heart that there   10
Love faints from all the pain that he endures;
For in themselves, poor sorrowing sighs, they bear
Inscribed my gracious lady's lovely name
And also of her death so many words.

[A.M.]

[XL]

O pilgrims lost in thought* who seem to go
Your way with something absent on your mind,
Have you come here from such a distant land
As your strange bearing and appearance show?
For as you pass you do not weep; and so,
Even within the sorrowing city's bounds,
You walk like those who do not understand
The tribulation that afflicts it now.
If only you could stay a while to hear,
My sighing heart has made me sure of this: 10
That you would weep as you departed then.
This city lacks its Beatrice, its bliss;
And those poor words that one may speak of her
Have power to draw tears from other men.

[A.M.]

135

[XLI]

Beyond the circling* of the widest sphere
Passes the sigh that issues from my heart:
A new intelligence that Love imparts
With weeping strives to draw him ever higher.
When he attains the goal of his desire,
He sees a woman honoured there whose light
Shines forth with such a splendour that the sight
Compels the pilgrim spirit to gaze on her.
The way he sees her makes him speak of this
In words too deep for me to understand,   10
Sent to the sorrowing heart that bids him tell.
I know he speaks of the most gracious one,
For he repeats the name of Beatrice
So I, dear ladies, understand him well.

[A.M.]

FROM
Convivio

[II]

Angels revolving the third sphere by thought,
Hear the articulation of my heart,
So strange I can unfold it to no others.
That sphere which moves according to your might –
Such elevated creatures as you are –
Is drawing me into my present state;
And so it would appear as only right
Discussion of my life should be with you.
Therefore I beg you give me your attention.
I shall explain my heart's bizarre condition,
Explain my soul, how she is weeping in it,
And how a spirit's in dispute with her,
Arriving on the rays of your own star.

What once gave life unto my grieving heart
Was a fine thought that used to make its way
So often to our Lord, where at his feet
It saw a lady shining gloriously,
Of whom it used to speak to me so sweetly
That my soul said: "I also would go there."
But now one comes who puts my soul to flight,
And lords it over me, and with such power
The trembling of my heart is all too clear.
This makes me see a lady and declare:
"Who wishes to experience heavenly bliss
Must gaze and gaze into this lady's eyes,
If he be not afraid of grievous sighs."

The humble thought who used to speak to me
About an angel who is crowned in heaven
Now meets an overwhelming adversary.
The soul laments, still grieving for the thought,

And says: "Alas, how that thought flees away,
Who was compassionate, consoling me!"
And she, my troubled soul, says of my eyes:
"Unhappy hour when such a lady saw them!
Why did they not believe me when I spoke?
Because I said: 'Yes, in her eyes there dwells
The very one who slays such as I am!'
But I had no advantage from the warning:
They gazed at her who makes me die of gazing."

"You are not dead, and yet you are bewildered,
Our soul, who live in so much lamentation,"
So speaks a gentle little spirit of love;
"For that fair lady whose great power you feel
Has now transformed you and your life so far,
And so abased you, you are full of fear!
But see how humble and how kind she is,
For all her greatness, courteous and wise:
Determine now to see her as your lady!
If you do not deceive yourself, you'll see
The beauty of such elevated marvels
As will cause you to say: 'Lord Love, my lord,
Do what you will, beholding your handmaid.'"

Canzone, I believe there will be few
Who come to understand your meaning fully,
So well-worked are your words and difficult.
So if it ever happens that by chance
You find yourself accounting to such people
As do not seem to see your meaning clearly,
Well then I beg you to be comforted,
My newcome darling, and suggest to them:
"At least reflect how beautiful I am!"

[J.G.N.]

FROM

The Divine Comedy

[*Inferno* V]

This is one of the most famous episodes in the Divine Comedy,
and has itself become part of the literature of romantic love.
Dante has left Limbo behind: now all the shades he meets have
damned themselves by their own actions. This second circle
contains the lustful. Virgil names some of these spirits, all of
them more or less legendary people. But then Dante speaks
to two people who had certainly existed and died during his
lifetime – Paolo Malatesta and Francesca da Rimini.

…I started: "Poet, I would be inclined
   To talk with those two who go yoked together
   And seem to be so light upon the wind."
Then he to me: "You try it when those two
   Have come much nearer. Beg them by that love
   Which drives them on, and they will turn to you."
Once they were blown towards us by the wind,
   I spoke: "O terribly tormented souls,   80
   Come here and speak to us, if that's not banned!"
And just as doves, attracted by desire
   Into their nest, their wings outspread and still,
   Glide with a clear intention through the air,
So these two left the throng where Dido was,
   And came to us through that foul atmosphere,
   Such was the power of my affectionate cries.
"O living being, so gracious and so good
   That you come visiting, through pitch-black air,
   Us who once stained this world of ours with blood, 90
Oh, if the Lord of all were but our friend,
   We would appeal to Him to give you peace,
   Since you show sympathy with our sad end.
And anything you wish to talk about,
   Whatever it is, we'll talk of it with you,
   In these few moments while the storm is mute.

I must explain my native city lies
   Upon that seacoast where the Po descends
   To the calm sea with all its tributaries.*
Love, kindling quickly in the noble heart,   100
   Seized him: he was enamoured of this body
   Killed in a way from which I suffer yet.*
Love, who insists all loved ones must requite
   Their lovers, seized me so with love's enjoyment
   That, as you see, love does not leave me yet.
Love chose a single death for both of us.
   Caïna* waits for him who took our lives."
   Such were the words of hers which came across.
I, when I'd heard these stricken souls, inclined
   My head, and for a long time held it down.   110
   At length the poet asked: "What's in your mind?"
Then I replied to him and said: "Alas!
   How many pleasant thoughts, and how much ardour
   Have brought this wretched pair to such a pass!"
And then once more I turned to them to speak
   And said: "Francesca, seeing how you suffer
   Makes me weep tears of sympathy and grief.
But tell me: in the time of gentle sighs,
   By what and in what way did Love permit you
   To recognize your dubious desires?"   120
She said: "There is no greater wretchedness
   Than calling back to mind a happy time
   In misery – your teacher* too knows this.
But, if you want to understand the root
   Cause of our love – it seems you really want to –
   I'll tell you, though I weep describing it.
We were reading one day for delectation
   Of Lancelot and how love held him close.*
   We were alone and quite without suspicion.
At several points that reading drew our eyes   130
   Together, drained the colour from our cheeks.

But one point only took us by surprise.
When we read how the smile of the belovèd
   Was kissed by such a celebrated lover,*
   This one,* from whom I never will be severed,
Kissed me upon the mouth, trembling all over.
   That book's a pander, and the man who wrote it:
   And on that day we read in it no further."

[J.G.N.]

[*Purgatory* II]

Dante and Virgil have just arrived at the foot of Purgatory.
Suddenly they notice a white light on the horizon, which rapidly
grows brighter and more distinct. This is one of God's angels,
bringing the souls of the saved to Purgatory in a boat. The new
arrivals notice that Dante is breathing, and they crowd around
him in wonder. One of these spirits is the singer and composer
Casella, an old friend of Dante.

The spirits, who had gathered what it meant
   That I was breathing – I was still alive –
   Had turned quite pale in their astonishment.
As people, hungry for good tidings, rush   70
   Around an olive-bearing messenger,*
   And no one hesitates to shove and push,
So everybody there, each happy soul,
   Stood gazing at my face, as though forgetting
   To go and make themselves more beautiful.*
And then I noticed one of them, who came
   Up to embrace me, and with such affection
   That he moved me to do the very same.
Oh shades, in all but your appearance, vain!
   Three times I clasped my hands behind him, and   80
   Three times I brought them to my breast again.
Wonder, I think, was what my face displayed,
   So that the shade drew back a little, smiling,
   And I pressed forward, following his lead.
He told me gently that I should hold back:
   And then I realized who he was, and begged him
   To pause a moment so that we might talk.
He answered me: "Because you had my love
   While bound in flesh, and have it now I'm freed,
   I'll pause; but why do you walk here, alive?"   90
"Casella,* friend, to come another time

146

To where I am," I said, "I make this journey;*
  But why are you deprived of so much time?"*
He said: "I have been done no injury,
  Though he who carries whom and when he pleases*
  Had several times refused to carry me,
Since his is fashioned by a will that's fair.*
  Nevertheless, for three months he has taken
  All wishing to embark, without demur.*
So he, when I'd arrived upon the shore,   100
  There where the River Tiber meets salt water,*
  Kindly received me as a passenger.
He is now winging to that mouth again,
  For it is there that all souls always gather,
  Unless they sink down to the Acheron."*
I answered: "If no legislation here
  Bans use or memory of those loving songs
  Which always fully solaced my desire,
I beg you sing them, and refresh somewhat
  My soul which, since it travelled with my body   110
  To reach this place, is utterly tired out!"
"Love who is talking with me in my mind..."*
  So he began to sing, and sang so sweetly
  That I still hear the sweetness of that sound.
My master then, and I, and all that band
  Around the singer seemed so well contented
  As nothing else could ever come to mind.

[J.G.N.]

[*Purgatory* XXX]

As Dante is being led through the Earthly Paradise, he sees a
procession, consisting of twenty-four elders and a chariot, which
stops in front of him. This is followed by a hundred people sing-
ing from within the chariot, using the words which welcomed
Christ into Jerusalem: they scatter lilies in abundance. Inside
this cloud of flowers a woman appears, wearing a white veil, a
green mantle and a dress of bright red.

Before now I have seen at break of day
   The eastern heavens glowing rosy-red
   And all the rest one blue serenity,
And seen the sun's face at its birth, but shaded,
   So that with all the intervening vapour
   The eye for long was able to sustain it:
Just so, within a flower-engendered cloud
   Rising and falling from the hands of angels
   To drift within the chariot and outside,   30
In a white veil, and olive-garlanded,
   A lady appeared to me, mantled in green,
   Her dress beneath the mantle flaming-red.*
My spirit now – for all the length of time
   Which had gone by since merely in her presence
   I shook with awe till I was overcome,
Without more knowledge which the eyes can give,
   Through hidden virtue coming out of her –
   Felt the great potency of ancient love.*
The instant that my eyes were stricken by   40
   That mighty power which had already pierced me
   Before my early boyhood had gone by,
I turned round to the left with all the trust
   A child has running up towards his mother
   When he's afraid or otherwise distressed,
To say to Virgil: "There is not one dram

Of blood now left in me that does not tremble:
    I know the tokens of the ancient flame";*
But Virgil had left us. Oh, the deprivation
    Of Virgil, dearest father, and that Virgil   50
    To whom I gave myself for my salvation!
All our first mother lost out of her keeping*
    Was insufficient now to keep my cheeks,
    Though washed in dew,* from being streaked with
    weeping.
"Dante, though Virgil has just disappeared,
    You must not weep yet, you must not weep yet,
    For you must weep beneath another sword."*
Now, like an admiral on prow or stern
    Who moves along the decks to check the sailors
    Serving on other ships and cheer them on: 60
So on the left side of the chariot,
    When I turned round at hearing my name spoken
    (Which here, here only I'm obliged to note),*
I saw the lady who first appeared to me
    Under the veil of the angelic welcome
    Direct across the stream her eyes to me.
Although the veil which came down from her head,
    Encircled by the foliage of Minerva,
    Would not allow her to be quite descried,
Regal of bearing, rigorous, steadfast,   70
    She recommenced like someone who, when speaking,
    Has kept her warmest words until the last:
"Look at me well! For I am Beatrice.
    How did you ever come to climb the Mountain?
    Did you not know here is man's happiness?

[J.G.N.]

149

[*Paradise* XXX]

Having journeyed through Paradise to the Empyrean, Dante turns to Beatrice, who is ever more beautiful. Unable to find words to express her beauty, he imagines that only God can perceive that beauty fully.

Perhaps six thousand miles away high noon
  Is blazing, and this world of ours already
  Casting its shadow almost on a plane,*
And heaven's atmosphere, so high above,
  Begins to change, so that the fainter stars
  Are being lost to sight on our low earth,
And as the brightest handmaid* of the sun
  Advances, heaven closes gradually
  All of its lights, down to the loveliest one.
Just so the angelic circle which rejoices   10
  For ever round the Point which dazzled me,
  And looks embraced by that which it embraces,
Little by little faded from my sight,
  Till lack of vision and my love constrained me
  To turn my eyes to Beatrice as a light.
If all that I have ever said of her
  Were integrated in one act of praise,
  It would not be enough to serve me here.
The beauty that I saw transcends so wholly
  All human understanding, I believe   20
  Only its Maker can enjoy it fully.
At this pass I am vanquished, I confess,
  More than at any instant in his work
  Comic or tragic poet ever was;
For, as the sun strikes on the weakest vision,
  Just so the memory of that sweet smile
  Plunges my intellect into confusion.

From the first day that ever I saw her face
   On earth,* until this sight, no obstacle
   Hindered the singing of my song like this;   30
But now I have no choice but to desist
   From following her beauty in my verses,
   As, at his wit's end, every artist must.

[J.G.N.]

[*Paradise* XXXIII]

In the final canto of Paradise, St Bernard, along with Beatrice and the other saints, prays for Dante. St Bernard then tells Dante to lift his eyes, and the poet experiences a beatific vision, which he struggles to express in words.

From that point what I saw was in excess
    Of anything that words can say, while even
    The memory falters at such overplus.
Like someone who sees something in his dreams
    And waking finds the passion that it roused
    Is with him still, though nothing seen remains,   60
Just so am I: my vision is in flight,
    While all the sweetness that was born of it
    Remains with me, distilled into my heart.
Like that, the snow is melted in the sun –
    Like that, upon the wind and drifting leaves,
    The Sibyl's oracles are swiftly gone.*
O Light Supreme, so elevated, far
    Above our mortal understanding, bring
    Back to my mind somewhat of what I saw
And give such vigour to this tongue of mine   70
    That I may leave but one spark of Your glory
    Behind me for the peoples yet unborn,
Which, part-returning to my memory,
    And echoing a little in these lines,
    May give some concept of Your victory.
I think the keenness of the living ray
    I underwent then would have left me dazzled
    Had I presumed to turn my eyes away.
And I remember that I grew more bold,
    Because of this, to endure it, till my gaze   80
    United with the Everlasting Good.

O grace abounding and through which I dared
  To fix my gaze on the Eternal Light
  So that no atom of my sight was spared!
In that profundity I saw – in-gathered,
  And bound by love into a single volume –
  All that throughout the universe is scattered:*
Substances, accidents,* how they relate
  In interpenetration, and so fused
  That what I say shines but a feeble light.   90
The universal structure of this knot
  Is what I know I saw, because I feel,
  While I am speaking, greater joy in it.
One instant brings me greater memory loss
  Than five-and-twenty centuries since Neptune
  Dumbfounded saw the Argo's shadow pass!*
Like him my mind was held in its amaze
  To gaze intently, fixedly, unmoving,
  With always more encouragement to gaze.
Before that Light one alters so that it   100
  Would be impossible one should consent
  To turn away for any other sight...

[J.G.N.]

A SELECTION OF POEMS
ATTRIBUTED
TO DANTE ALIGHIERI

Love and the Lady Lagia, Guido and I   1
Can thank Sir Somebody who has undone
The ties that bound us; you know who I mean
(I'd rather not remember, don't ask me).
Since then these three have been content to be
Unbound, although the service they have done
To Love was no less worthy than my own,
Who pictured him as like a god on high.
Let Love be thanked, for it was first his part
To see the truth, and the wise lady then   10
Who chose that moment to take back her heart,
And Guido who is now completely free.
And I, should I fall in his power again,
You won't believe how happy I would be.

[A.M.]

I feel my spirit weeping inwardly,   1
Just as these eyes are made to weep its woe,
And still it says: "Alas, I did not know
The strength of her who triumphs over me;
In her the very face of Love I see,
More cruel than ever with an angry brow
That seems to say: 'What's this? Where are you now,
Locked in a body that is doomed to die?'
Before my eyes Love opens up a book
In which I read of all those torments where   10
Men see the path that leads them to their death.
And then he tells me: 'Wretched man, you look
Upon the sentence that condemns us both
And that her loveliness has written there.'"

[A.M.]

Have you not marked a man whose sorrows weigh   1
Upon his weeping features, deathly pale?
If not, then see him now and do not fail
To heed him, for your honour's sake, I pray.
He goes along sunk deep in his dismay,
Complexioned like a corpse, his eyes so full
Of pain that all his strength will not avail
To make him lift them from the trodden way.
And if he should receive some pitying glance
His heart is racked with tears, his soul with cries   10
Forced out by grief that he can not endure;
And, were it not that he takes flight at once,
He calls on you so loudly in his sighs
That men would say: "We know his murderer."

[A.M.]

She who has made me wander full of care   1
Carries the power of Love high in her face,
Which reawakens the same gentle force
Within men's hearts if it lies hidden there.
She has so overwhelmed my mind with fear,
Since in her eyes I saw the sweet lord's grace
And knew his power, that now I take my place
Close by her side, yet dare not look at her.
And if by any chance I fix my gaze
Upon those eyes I find there my salvation   10
That with the intellect I cannot seize.
Then are my vital spirits so put down
That the soul, even as it breathes out sighs,
Resolves to leave the heart and soon be gone.

[A.M.]

Note on the Text

The translations in this volume are based upon the following Italian editions: *Rime di Dante Alighieri*, ed. Gianfranco Contini (Turin: Einaudi, 1995), *Vita Nuova*, ed. Michele Barbi for the Società Dantesca Italiana (Florence: Bemporad, 1932), *Convivio*, ed. Giorgio Inglese (Milan: Rizzoli, 1993) and *La Divina Commedia*, ed. Natalino Sapegno, 3 vols. (Florence: La Nuova Italia, 1985).

Notes

p. 5, *Dante da Maiano*: Dante da Maiano was one of the many who responded to the first poem in Dante's *Vita Nuova*.

p. 12, *Ovid's prescription's... love's cure*: In his *Remedia Amoris*, Ovid (43 BC–18 AD) suggests the ways by which love may be "cured".

p. 14, *I come... naked maid*: See the poem which follows.

p. 14, *To clothe her*: If we knew this poem's addressee the interpretation of the metaphor (to set to music, to comment upon, to copy in a fair hand) would be easier.

p. 19, *the Garisenda Tower*: A leaning tower in Bologna famous because, when a cloud passes over, it appears to be toppling (*Inferno* XXXI, 136–38).

p. 20, *Guido*: Guido Cavalcanti (*c.*1260–1300), the "first of my friends", as Dante says in his *Vita Nuova*.

p. 20, *Lapo*: A friend of Dante and a poet.

p. 20, *Monna Vanna, Monna Lagia*: The ladies of Guido and Lapo respectively.

p. 20, *the thirtieth lady*: A verse epistle of Dante's, which is not extant, mentioned and numbered the sixty most beautiful ladies in Florence; since Beatrice was ninth, it seems that they were not numbered in order of beauty.

p. 21, *Clothing*: Presumably a musical setting, see *Rime* v, 18.

p. 28, *Meuccio's*: Probably the poet Meuccio Tolomei of Siena.

p. 28, *some things of his which he holds dear*: Poems.

p. 30, *Into your hands... dying throes*: See Luke 23:46: "And when Jesus had cried with a loud voice, he said, Father, into thy hands I commend my spirit: and having said this, he gave up the ghost."

p. 30, *Do unto me according to your word*: Mark 14:36: "And he said, Abba, Father, all things are possible unto thee; take away this cup from me: nevertheless not what I will, but what thou wilt." Also Luke 1:38: "And Mary said, 'Behold the handmaid of the Lord; be it unto me according to thy word.'"

p. 34, *That name, so sweet, which makes my heart so bitter*: A play upon the name "Beatrice", which suggests "bringer of blessedness".

p. 45, *Angels... thought*: The first line of one of the poems (*Voi che 'ntendendo il terzo ciel movete*) which Dante comments upon in his *Convivio* (see pp. 139–40). The third of the nine heavenly spheres in the Ptolemaic system was that of Venus, goddess of love.

p. 46, *Sweet rhymes*: The "my words" of the previous poem, to which this one is a palinode.

p. 46, *One*: A reference to the previous poem.

p. 47, *my beloved master*: Love personified, who is also "The fountain of fine speech" in line 12.

p. 48, *XXXIV*: This and the following two poems may well be connected with an incident in *Purgatory* XXXI, 58–60, where Beatrice reproaches Dante for having been led astray by the love of a young girl (*pargoletta*):

> You never should have let your either wing
> Flag, for some further blows from some young girl
> Or any trumpery ephemeral thing.

p. 50, *and die that others might the danger shun*: The statement of Caiaphas (John 11:50): "Consider that it is expedient for us, that one man should die for the people, and that the whole nation perish not."

p. 50, *A pearl... influence of a star*: The value of a precious stone was thought to be the result of the influence of a star upon it.

p. 51, *XXXVII*: The opening lines of this poem recall the final line of the *Divine Comedy*: "*l'amor che move il sole e l'altre stelle*" ("The love which moves the sun and all the stars").

p. 51, *As water... kindles flame*: A reference to the fact that water in a glass vessel acts as a lens.

p. 54, *XXXVIII*: The understanding of this difficult poem may be facilitated by a stanza-by-stanza summary:

St. 1: The poet grieves because he is weakened almost to death by love; however, love does not assault him against his will; he grieves because his strength does not correspond to his will, which would be to suffer longer; at least his will deserves the reward of the longer life that her eyes could confer.

St. 2: Those eyes bring sweetness and love; if they are hidden, they bring loss not only to the poet but to the lady as well, because she will lose the service he would have given her – service which might paradoxically even include leaving her.

St. 3: This stanza develops the idea of service which does not depend on the lady's caprices and which remains service whether she accepts it or not: time will teach her better.

St. 4: Love for the lady leads the poet to another love, one which leads to noble action; in this sense his service is the reward he receives from her; nevertheless, he *is* a servant, because he is entirely devoted to her good, not his own.

St. 5: Only Love could confer dignity on the state of belonging to someone who gives no love in return; each time the poet sees her he finds fresh beauty, and so Love's power is increased; when he does not see her, Love continues to educate him through suffering and delight.

St. 6: The song should be modest and avoid bad company.

St. 7: The song is sent to the "three least vicious men" in Florence, the third of whom may well be Dante's friend, the poet Guido Cavalcanti, who is told that he should not feel ashamed to abandon evil companions.

p. 59, *band*: A veil.

p. 60, *Cino da Pistoia*: Cino dei Sigibuldi of Pistoia (*c.*1270–1336/7) was a prolific writer of lyrics, highly praised by both Dante and Petrarch.

p. 60, *the green... the black*: A young woman dressed in green is contrasted with another woman dressed in black.

p. 61, *I have once... no fruit*: Apollo (the sun), whose son Phaethon drowned in the River Po ("the stream of Lombardy"), can make a rootless tree turn green, but cannot make it bear fruit.

p. 62, *wrong... shut out*: This suggests that the poem was written from exile.

p. 63, *unless your faith has crumbled there*: This recalls the theological distinction between faith and good works as means to salvation.

p. 64, *A fresh young maid*: A poem, but we do not know which one.

p. 64, *Brother Alberts*: Wiseacres, in allusion to the learned Dominican St Albert the Great (1193–1280).

p. 64, *Master Giano*: It would fit the attitude taken in the poem to its (now unknown) addressee if this were a notoriously stupid person.

p. 65, *XLIII*: This and the three poems which follow it form a distinct group known, because of their recurrent image of stone, as the *rime petrose* (stony poems). The woman concerned may be identical with the *pargoletta* of XXXIV–XXXVI.

p. 65, *heaven's wheel*: The motion of the heavenly bodies.

p. 65, *those clear twins*: The zodiacal sign of Gemini.

p. 65, *love's star*: Venus.

p. 65, *the cold planet*: Saturn.

p. 65, *seven*: The seven planets (including the sun and moon) of medieval astronomy. Dante's details are exact and indicate December 1296 as the date he is alluding to, although that does not necessarily coincide with when the poem was written.

p. 65, *the seven freezing stars*: The constellation known as the Great Bear or the Plough.

p. 66, *the power of the Ram*: The sun is in the sign of the Ram (Aries) at the spring equinox.

p. 68, *XLIV*: The first known use in Italian of the sestina, a verse form of six six-line stanzas having the same end words in different orders and concluding with a tercet containing all of them; it is particularly appropriate for suggesting obsession and paralysis.

p. 72, *A form unthought-of in all earlier time*: A reference to the verse form used in this poem, a development of the sestina to make it even more complicated.

p. 73, *XLVI*: This poem stands out as a new departure in its complex syntax and concrete imagery, and the overall hardness of tone.

p. 74, *That murdered Dido triumphs over me*: In the *Aeneid*, Dido, Queen of Carthage, kills herself with the sword of Aeneas, who has abandoned her.

p. 76, *XLVII*: This is, apart from the *Divine Comedy*, Dante's greatest poem of exile. He draws strength from the fact that the moral values he cherishes are exiled also: it is the fate of worth to be banished. These values are allegorized as noble ladies whose dignity is in inverse proportion to their shameful condition.

p. 77, *her*: Natural Law, inborn in human beings at the Creation.

p. 77, *the one*: Human laws, derived from natural law, which itself derives from that righteousness (l. 35) inherent in the nature of things.

p. 79, *falcons feathered white*: A reference to the White Guelfs, the Florentine faction which opposed Papal influence.

p. 79, *the sable hounds*: The Black Guelfs, who supported the Pope.

p. 80, *Lord*: This poem is a prayer.

p. 80, *her*: Justice.

p. 80, *the man*: Probably Pope Clement V (1264–1314), who transferred the Papal See to Avignon, the notorious "Babylonian Captivity" (1309–77).

p. 80, *the chief Tyrant*: King Philip the Fair of France (1268–1314).

p. 81, *XLIX*: This is sometimes called the "*canzone* of liberality", but in fact only stanzas 4–6 deal directly with that theme. Sexual licence and avarice seem to be linked as evidence of the world's moral decline.

p. 82, *double loss*: The loss of virtue and the descent into servitude.

p. 82, *covered by a veil*: The women to whom the poem is addressed will not understand a message that is "veiled" in allegory; in addition, since it was women who wore veils, there may be intended the generalization that women rarely understand allegory.

p. 83, *our light*: The light of understanding which would enable us to judge how the wealth left over at death might be reapportioned.

p. 84, *he evades the snare*: The image is of a hawk being lured by the falconer.

p. 84, *charity*: In the sense of "giving".

p. 85, *Bianca or Giovanna or Countess*: Most likely the names suggest, respectively, *beautiful*, *wise* and *courteous*: the use of three names suggests that there is more than one woman who is perfect and therefore fit to receive the poem.

p. 86, *death*: The literal death of the loved one.

p. 86, *two extremes*: Probably cold and heat, either of which can kill.

p. 86, *black and white*: This is ambiguous: a clear allusion to the new woman's eyes, but also to the Black and White Guelf factions in Pistoia and Florence.

p. 86, *both in and out*: In and out of love; also in Florence and then out of it as an exile.

p. 87, *my ninth revolution of the sun*: Dante was nine years old when he first met and fell in love with Beatrice.

p. 88, *Marchese Moroello Malaspina*: A benefactor of both Cino and Dante.

p. 88, *The perfect gold… noble mind*: Love.

p. 88, *An evil thorn*: Malaspina literally means "evil thorn"; the lady alluded to may well therefore be a member of that family.

p. 88, *And there… me suffer*: The tone is presumably playful.

p. 88, *the rugged mount*: The lady's obduracy.

p. 88, *Yet still… a fount*: This is cryptic: if "my master" (l. 12) alludes to Moroello, then this line may allude to some previous tangible gift of his to Cino, perhaps hospitality or even money; this would of course alter our interpretation of line 2. Line 14 is bound to call to mind Moses bringing water out of a rock in the desert (Exodus 17:1–6), but this does not make Cino's sense any clearer to us.

p. 91, *Exiled me… land*: Cino was exiled from Pistoia from 1301 to 1306.

p. 92, *LIII*: Written from exile, and probably the last poem Dante wrote before his *Divine Comedy*.

p. 93, *where she truly dwells*: Herself as distinct from her image.

p. 94, *This outlaw from your court*: The lady (possibly Beatrice) who is the subject of this poem.

p. 99, *III… For every gentle heart*: Numbers indicate relevant sections of the *Vita Nuova* as given in the Barbi edition. This is the first of many premonitions of the death of Beatrice. Many contemporary poets, including Guido Cavalcanti, replied to Dante's invitation to interpret his dream.

p. 100, *O all of you who pass*: Dante has addressed his attentions and some poems to the so-called Screen Lady in order to conceal his love for Beatrice. Now that she is leaving the city he feels obliged to "write something sorrowful about her departure" to maintain the deception. But the perceptive reader, he tells us, will understand that Beatrice is "the direct cause of certain words".

p. 101, *Weep, lovers*: Written after the funeral of a young lady who had been the friend of Beatrice. The mourning Beatrice represents Love "in his own true form".

p. 102, *Death, churlish villain*: A second poem on the same topic. The apostrophe denouncing death is common in poetry belonging to the "complaint" tradition. The first twelve lines are deliberately harsh in sound and awkward in syntax.

p. 103, *Riding along*: On a journey that takes him near to where the Screen Lady now lives, Dante meets Love, who instructs him to find a new Screen Lady. Love appears as a dejected traveller, almost a mirror image of the poet.

p. 104, *Ballad, I pray you*: Hearing that Dante's attentions to the second Screen Lady have gone beyond the bounds of courtesy, Beatrice denies the poet her greeting. Urged by Love, he decides to abandon subterfuge and sends a poem to plead his case.

p. 106, *I needs must... lady Pity*: Lady Pity has proved an enemy in that she has neglected the poet ever since Beatrice withdrew her greeting.

p. 107, *When other ladies mock me:* This and the following two sonnets refer to an episode at a wedding where Dante has been seized by a fit of fainting and trembling at the sight of Beatrice, who then joins the other ladies in mocking his weakness.

p. 110, *Ladies that have intelligence of love*: The poet announces that he will change the subject matter of his work from his own sufferings to the praise of Beatrice.

Dante obviously attached great importance to this *canzone*. In *Purgatory* (XXIV, 49–60) we hear the poet Bonagiunta da Lucca cite it as central to the poetic movement known as the *dolce stil novo*: it is also mentioned in *De vulgari eloquentia* (II, 8), where Dante argues for the *canzone* as the supreme form of vernacular lyric poetry.

p. 110, *I will not... you*: The poet will adopt a light manner designed for his female audience rather than the high style appropriate to his subject. This humble stance is a conventional rhetorical ploy and is soon belied by the exalted tone of the *canzone*.

p. 110, *Pity alone remains... part*: Pity pleads with God to let Beatrice remain on earth a little longer.

p. 110, *Your hope will... blessed*: The lines are hyperbolic: the celestial destiny of Beatrice puts her at a vast distance from the poet, but even if he were to end in hell, he would still know the consolation of having seen her.

p. 111, *young and plain*: The supposedly humble style of the poem (ll. 9–14) now serves as a guarantee of its sincerity.

p. 113, *Love and the noble heart*: The line echoes Guido Guinizzelli's celebrated "Love always comes to the noble heart", considered as a founding text of the *dolce stil novo*.

p. 113, *he sleeps on*: Love is present in the noble heart as potentiality, waiting to be transformed into act by the advent of virtuous beauty.

p. 114, *My lady's eyes... looks upon*: Beatrice does more than transform potentiality into act: like God, she creates that potentiality in the first place.

p. 115, *You ladies who proceed*: The poet meets a group of ladies coming from the funeral of Beatrice's father. He questions them about her grief. The subsequent sonnet ("Can you be he") provides their answer.

p. 117, *A lady moved by pity*: During an illness the poet has a premonitory dream of the death of Beatrice.

p. 118, *I saw strange things... fear*: These details recall the death of Christ in the gospels of Matthew and Luke; see also Revelation 6:12–14. The narrow space of a room opens up to cosmic perspectives, reflecting the way in which the poet's personal drama is related to the universal drama of man's salvation.

p. 118, *I raised... Hosanna*: Manna feeds the Israelites in the desert and is typologically related to Christ as the "bread of life" (John 6:31–35). The Psalmist raises his eyes to the hills (Psalms 121:1), and the small cloud traditionally represents the ascending soul.

p. 119, *false fantasies*: We are reminded here (and at ll. 43–44) that the events foreshadowed in the dream had not yet come to pass when the poem was supposedly written.

p. 120, *Within my heart*: The poet feels the old familiar tremor (see *Purgatory* XXX, 46–48) at the approach of Beatrice (Bice), preceded by Vanna (Giovanna), also known as Primavera. In the prose comment Dante reminds us that the name Giovanna derives from John the Baptist who preceded the True Light of Christ.

p. 120, *Is Love because... me*: In VIII, 10, Love's "own true form" was that of Beatrice. Now Beatrice also assumes the name of Love.

p. 121, *With such a gentle*: The first of two sonnets celebrating the way the God-given grace and beauty of Beatrice transforms the community in which she lives.

p. 123, *So long has Love been lord*: The first stanza of a poem that Dante left incomplete on hearing of the death of Beatrice.

p. 124, *These eyes that... sigh*: It is only when the first violence of grief has passed that verbal expression becomes possible and necessary.

p. 124, *Excess of cold or heat*: In medieval medical theory, inherited from the Greeks, death occurred from an imbalance between the body's four constituent qualities of Hot, Cold, Dry and Wet, which are related to the four elements of Earth (dry and cold), Water (cold and wet), Fire (hot and dry), Air (wet and hot).

p. 124, *full of grace*: Recalling "*Ave gratia plena*", the Vulgate's version of the Angel Gabriel's words to Mary (Luke 1:28).

p. 126, *your sisters*: His other poems; a fairly common metaphor.

p. 127, *Come, O ye gentle hearts*: This and the following poem ("When I recall, alas") were, Dante tells us, written at the request of the brother of Beatrice, who asked him to compose something for a lady who had just died. Dante, of course, realizes that he is speaking of Beatrice. The situation recalls the episode of the Screen Lady.

p. 129, *Into my mind there came*: Some prominent citizens interrupt Dante while he is working on a drawing of an angel. He excuses his failure to greet them by the fact that it is the first anniversary of the death of Beatrice. The two beginnings suggest Dante's desire to convince the reader that he is offering an exact transcription of poems composed at the time of the events they describe.

p. 130, *With my own eyes*: The first of five sonnets dealing with a gentle lady who takes pity on Dante's distress. Only in 'Alas, the force of many sighs' (XXXIX) does he finally realize that he is not capable of returning her love.

p. 135, *O pilgrims lost in thought*: Dante addresses the pilgrims who pass through Florence on their way to Rome. The association of lover and pilgrim was to become a commonplace of Petrarchism, but here the image suggests the analogy between Beatrice and Christ.

p. 136, *Beyond the circling*: A final vision of Beatrice in glory. The "widest sphere" is the Primum Mobile, which imparts movement to the eight other spheres. Beyond it lies the motionless Empyrean, which is the realm of eternity.

p. 144, *O living being... all its tributaries*: The speaker is Francesca da Rimini. Born in Ravenna, she was married to

Gianciotto Malatesta, but fell in love with his brother Paolo. Her husband came upon the guilty pair and killed them.

p. 144, *Killed in a way from which I suffer yet*: Not only was her death violent, but it allowed her no time to repent.

p. 144, *Caïna*: A zone of the lowest circle of the Inferno (XXXII), reserved for those who betray their relatives. It is named after Cain, who murdered his brother Abel (Gen. 4:8).

p. 144, *your teacher*: Virgil.

p. 144, *Lancelot and how love held him close*: The adulterous love of Lancelot for Guinevere, the wife of his lord King Arthur.

p. 145, *the smile of the belovèd… celebrated lover*: Guinevere was kissed by Lancelot.

p. 145, *This one*: Paolo.

p. 146, *an olive-bearing messenger*: An olive branch was a sign that the news was good.

p. 146, *To go and make themselves more beautiful*: To purify themselves from the last traces of sin.

p. 146, *Casella*: A man of whom little is known, except that he sang and set words to music.

p. 147, *to come another time… this journey*: Dante knows that the purpose of his journey is to make him worthy of salvation.

p. 147, *deprived of so much time*: Time to complete his purgation. Dante, who must have known that Casella had been dead for a while, is surprised to find him arriving only now at the island of Purgatory. All those in Purgatory feel the need to complete their purgation as quickly as possible.

p. 147, *he who carries whom and when he pleases*: The angel who ferries the souls to Purgatory.

p. 147, *his is fashioned by a will that's fair*: His will is conformed to God's. No reason is given for the angel's previous refusals.

p. 147, *for three months… without demur*: Since the Christmas of 1299, when the Pope declared the start of the

Jubilee Year of 1300, with the possibility of gaining plenary indulgences for the dead.

p. 147, *where the River Tiber meets salt water*: Where the Tiber flows into the Tyrrhenian Sea.

p. 147, *there that all souls... Acheron*: The souls of the saved assemble at the mouth of the Tiber, and the damned on the bank of Acheron.

p. 147, *Love who is talking with me in my mind*: The first line of a *canzone* by Dante which is discussed in the third section of his *Convivio*.

p. 148, *white veil... mantle flaming-red*: The colours of the veil, the mantle and the dress allude respectively to faith, hope and charity. The olive garland is a sign of peace; also the olive was sacred to Minerva (Pallas Athena), goddess of wisdom (see l. 68 below).

p. 148, *My spirit now... ancient love*: "Since my birth the sun had already returned nine times to the same point in its revolution, when there first appeared to me the glorious lady of my memory" (*Vita Nuova* 1).

p. 149, *There is not... the ancient flame*: Aeneid IV, 22.

p. 149, *All our first mother lost out of her keeping*: All the pleasures of the Garden of Eden, lost by Eve.

p. 149, *washed in dew*: At the foot of Mount Purgatory (see *Purg.* I, 121–29).

p. 149, *another sword*: The knowledge of his sins.

p. 149, *Which here... obliged to note*: This, an apology for what might be construed as vanity, has also the effect of stressing that Dante is recording facts accurately.

p. 150, *Casting its shadow almost on a plane*: As the sun sinks the earth's shadow is lowered.

p. 150, *the brightest handmaid*: Aurora, the dawn.

p. 151, *the first day... on earth*: When he was nine years old.

p. 152, *The Sibyl's oracles are swiftly gone:* The Sibyl was a prophetess who wrote her prophecies on leaves which were easily scattered by the wind.

p. 153, *All that throughout the universe is scattered*: The source of everything is in God, and what holds it all together is love.

p. 153, *Substances, accidents*: Substances are things which exist in themselves; accidents are qualities which exist only in substances, differentiating them.

p. 153, *One instant... shadow pass*: The Argonauts' voyage to Colchis in quest of the Golden Fleece has left, after two and a half thousand years, more trace in the memory of mankind than the Beatific Vision has left in Dante's mind after one instant.

Extra Material

on

Dante Alighieri's

Love Poems

Dante Alighieri's Life

We know far more about Dante the man than we do about
Shakespeare, even though Shakespeare is three hundred years
closer to us. We know what Dante looked like from the several
similar portraits which survive (some of which may well be
contemporary), and from a detailed pen portrait by a fellow
Florentine writing only a short while after his subject's death:

> Our poet was of medium height, and after he came to maturity
> he bent somewhat as he walked, and his gait was grave and
> gentle. He was always dressed in good clothes of a fashion
> appropriate to his years. His face was long, his nose aquiline,
> his eyes rather big, his jaw large, and his lower lip protruded
> beyond the upper. His complexion was dark, his hair and beard
> thick, black and curly, and his expression was melancholy and
> thoughtful. (Giovanni Boccaccio, *Life of Dante*)

We know about his marriage, his children, and his close friend-
ships with men like the considerably older Brunetto Latini
and the slightly older and socially superior Guido Cavalcanti
($c.$1258–1300), from both of whom he learnt so much. His
public life – with first its civic responsibilities and then the
torment of the lack of those responsibilities after his perma-
nent exile from his native city – is well documented. There are
myths also, of course: it may not be strictly true that, when
he passed by in Verona, one woman declared that this was the
man who visited hell and another saw the proof of this in the
apparently singed beard and smoke-browned face; but even
such myths reveal that he was the sort of man around whom
myths gather. His views on an astonishing range of topics
and people are available to us: he does not disappear behind
his works as Shakespeare does. Shakespeare of course was a

177

dramatic writer, but then so was Dante in a way, especially in his chief work, his *Divina Commedia* (*Divine Comedy*). The difference is that Dante is himself part of his own drama, and not just in the same manner as, say, Chaucer is with his incidental self-mockery, but as the protagonist who is always there and never afraid of putting his oar in – one of the main reasons why we know so much about him.

Early Life in Florence   The Florence into which Dante was born in 1265 was a city only beginning on its progress towards the political and cultural dominance of Tuscany: indeed, five years before his birth, after the battle of Montaperti between Tuscan Ghibellines and Florentine Guelfs, the victorious Ghibellines were with difficulty dissuaded from razing the city to the ground. This is a sobering thought: it is hard to imagine what European culture would be like now without the influence of Florence, and just as hard to imagine European literature without Dante.

Dante's father was a reasonably successful businessman: the nature of his business is uncertain, but may well have involved usury (a foretaste perhaps of the later importance of Florentine banking), and the family were comfortably off. Dante had the usual formal education of his time, which involved Latin grammar, logic and rhetoric, followed by arithmetic, geometry, astronomy and music. Even the most cursory reading of his works, however, makes it apparent that his learning and, more importantly, his understanding, went far beyond the requirements of any formal education. In Florence he was able to benefit from the society of some of the most accomplished men of his time. He makes a striking comment on his education in the *Inferno*, when he comes across the shade of the diplomat, scholar and writer Brunetto Latini, damned for sodomy; even in such circumstances respect and gratitude demand to be expressed:

> ...still I have in mind, to my great pain,
> The dear, the kindly, the paternal image
> Of you who, in the world, time and again,
> Taught me how man becomes eternal...
> (*Inf.* xv, 82–85)

There is much of Dante in these few lines – his unflinching moral judgement (after all, it is in his poem that Brunetto is seen to be damned), his deep human sympathies and his strong desire (despite the overriding importance of his eternal destiny) for posthumous renown on earth.

His father's death in 1283 meant that Dante was placed under a guardian for several years until he came of age. However, he was old enough in 1289 to fight in the battle of Campaldino, where the Florentine Guelfs defeated the Ghibellines of Arezzo, so reversing the disaster of Montaperti; and he was also present some months later at the siege of Caprona, during an incursion into Pisan territory. There was never anything in Dante of the temperament which Milton was later to disparage as "a fugitive and cloistered virtue, unexercised and unbreathed, that never sallies out and sees her adversary" (*Areopagitica*): his unwillingness to walk away from a fight is as obvious in spiritual as in physical matters.

Dante married in 1285 a certain Gemma Donati, of whom *Marriage* we know little except that she bore him several children and did not follow him into exile. She seems to have had property of her own which could not be affected by the sentence issued against Dante, and since there was a family to provide for, remaining in Florence probably made good practical sense. Even Boccaccio, who strongly deprecated marriage for a scholar, had to admit that he had no evidence that Dante's marriage was worse than any other he knew of. Dante's children certainly kept in touch with their father till the end of his life, and two of his sons conscientiously gathered and preserved the various parts of the *Commedia* after his death.

According to Dante's own account, the most formative event *Beatrice* of his life occurred when, at the age of nine, he saw, at a festival, the little girl, some months younger than he was, who has been identified as Bice (Beatrice) Portinari. To say that he immediately fell and always remained in love with her is a feeble way of describing what was a lifelong obsession, often in the foreground and always in the background of his writings. Boccaccio discusses this event sympathetically in his *Life of Dante*, and a more detailed account of its consequences can be read in Dante's own *Vita Nuova* (*New Life*); but only a reading of the hundred cantos of the *Divina Commedia* reveals the full effect of this childhood event. Beatrice died at the age of twenty-four, and we can have no idea what she thought of it all, or even whether she had any awareness of her importance to Dante.

When Dante came of age, it was inevitable that he should *Political* play his part in the politics of Florence. The city was violently *Activities* disturbed by disputes between the aristocrats and the merchant class, among the aristocrats themselves, and also between the rival parties of the Ghibellines and Guelfs. This last conflict especially is one where the various interests are hard now to disentangle. Hostility between Guelfs and Ghibellines was not confined to

Florence, and it influenced that city's foreign policy as well as its internal affairs, as it had in the battles of Montaperti and Campaldino. Behind these party divisions, sometimes a long way behind, was the centuries-old struggle between the Pope, as the head of Western Christendom, and the Holy Roman Emperor, as at least the titular head of secular power in Europe. Conflict between the demands of religious conscience and civic duty is perennial; but this problem was aggravated throughout the Middle Ages by the papal claim to secular as well as religious power. As a gross oversimplification, it may be said that the Ghibellines favoured the Emperor and the Guelfs the Pope. Applying that simplification to Dante we can say that he began as a Guelf and ended as a philosophical Ghibelline, deploring the papal claims to secular power. A further complication is that the Guelf party in Florence was split into two – the Blacks and the Whites. This distinction may seem to us trivial, but it led to the second most decisive event in Dante's life. Reading of all this turmoil is likely to put one in mind of Max Beerbohm's humorous tale *Savonarola Brown*. The eponymous hero's play on the life of Savonarola contains, time and again and for no particular reason, the stage direction "Enter Guelfs and Ghibellines, fighting", followed after a while by "Exeunt Guelfs and Ghibellines, still fighting". It may well be that many at the time in Florence, including possibly Dante himself, found it difficult to know what was really going on. At any rate, in 1300 Dante, as one of the seven Priors (the governing body, elected for a period of only two months), in an attempt to pacify the city agreed to the exile of some of the leaders of the Black and White Guelfs, including his friend Guido Cavalcanti. In 1302 Dante as a White Guelf found himself condemned to death by the Blacks, and his property confiscated. Since he was out of the city when the sentence was pronounced, he preserved his life, but only at the cost of remaining in exile. Years later an offer came of safe return to Florence and the restitution of his property if he would admit the truth of the trumped-up charges against him: he spurned the offer.

Exile and death   Dante spent the rest of his life wandering from city to city in Italy, depending on the benevolence of patrons for his livelihood. Banishment came as a disaster to one who believed, as Dante so firmly did, that an individual's good was bound up with the good of his society. Although for a long time he entertained the hope of returning eventually to his native city, and even of being crowned with laurel in the place where he had been baptized (his beloved San Giovanni, the present-day Baptistery), in reality he fulfilled the prophecy which, with

hindsight, he put into the mouth of his ancestor Cacciaguida
when he met him in his *Paradiso*:

> You shall leave every single thing behind
> Which you hold dear; and this is but the first
> Arrow that exile shoots, and your first wound.
> You shall experience the bitterness
> Of eating strangers' bread, and feel how hard
> Going up and down another's staircase is.
> (*Par.* XVII, 55–60)

The places where he stayed included, among others, Forlì,
Verona, Arezzo, Treviso, Padua, Venice, Lunigiana, Lucca,
Verona again, and eventually Ravenna. It was there that he
completed his *Divine Comedy*, died in 1321, and was buried.

Dante Alighieri's Works

Dante was still in his teens when he first showed his poems to his
friends in Florence. Manuscript circulation was a common form
of publication in the days before printing, when books were few
and expensive; what was perhaps not so common was that Dante's
recipients included men who were themselves accomplished poets,
particularly Guido Cavalcanti: he cannot have lacked informed
criticism and encouragement. The drawback of this kind of
publication is that short poems, such as Dante's were at this
early stage, tend to get scattered, and the relationship between
them, and between them and other people's poems, tends to be
forgotten, and accurate dating is now hard to achieve.

Although no such collection was ever published in Dante's *Rime*
lifetime, *Rime* is the usual title given to editions of Dante's lyrics.
It is essentially a conglomeration of miscellaneous poems, writ-
ten by Dante over the whole course of his adult life. In his lyrical
poems Dante was always experimenting, trying out different
styles and often returning to rework, and develop further, old
styles he might well be expected to have gone beyond.

As a young man Dante inherited a dominant theme which
frequently had the merit of sophistication and subtlety, but just
as frequently suffered from a lack of variety: it sometimes seems
as if there was only one theme for a poet to treat. The ideal of
what is often called "courtly love", but is better described as *fin
amor* (refined love), had become fashionable in twelfth-century
Languedoc. It was clearly tenacious; indeed in a certain form
it survives today. This idealization of a loved woman, and the

expression of the refining effect that this had on her poet, was not always as limiting as one might think. It was usually written by men of affairs – and not simply love affairs – lawyers, diplomats, administrators; and with any of the poems of Dante's precursors there is always the possibility that the theme of love is being used allegorically for the expression of social or political concerns. Dante developed the theme in ways no one else could have imagined: even in his short poems there is a movement towards an allegory which goes well beyond erotic love and the times and places of party or office politics.

Vita Nuova   Dante's first book-length production, his *Vita Nuova* (*New Life*), was probably composed when he was nearly thirty. It is made up partly of poems which had been written years before, but which fitted in with the book's prose narrative and commentary; or perhaps they were poems he wished to preserve and which suggested the prose to him. It is in this book that Dante describes his first meeting with Beatrice and how it influenced his early life. We learn of the physical effects, tantamount to a form of illness, which his obsession had on him, how he tried to conceal the object of his passion by paying court to another lady, his joy at Beatrice's greeting and his anguish when that greeting was denied him, his suffering in sympathy with her when her father died; it is always the effect on Dante himself which his poems seem most interested in. The book can be read in many different ways. One of its most interesting features is that the poems tend to talk about themselves, and it is illuminating to read *Vita Nuova* as an *ars poetica*. Eventually Dante comes to a momentous decision – to concentrate on praising Beatrice; he even declares:

> ...if it should please Him by Whom all things live that my life should last for a few more years, I hope to write of her what has never been written of any woman.

Dante may or may not have had *The Divine Comedy* already in mind when he wrote those words; but it was in the *Comedy* that he achieved that astounding ambition.

De vulgari   Some time in his thirties Dante began writing his *De vulgari*
eloquentia   *eloquentia* (*Literature in the Vernacular*). That an essay which insists on the value of the vernacular should be written in Latin is itself an indication of why such an insistence was needed: the prestige of Latin as the language for serious matters survived long after Dante's time. Dante gives cogent reasons for valuing the vernacular: it is the language we all possess, it is more natural than Latin since we learn it at our mother's knee, and we learn it in a sense without trying

consciously to learn it – unlike Latin, which we have to obtain in an artificial way through a study of its grammar. Although he is talking of Italian, many of the issues he raises are applicable to any language, and this work retains its importance today despite its unfinished state. Dante attempts to identify which of the many vernaculars in Italy presents the language in its purest form, and he comes to the conclusion that it is one which has

> left its scent in every city but made its home in none... which belongs to every Italian city yet seems to belong to none, and against which the vernaculars of all the cities of the Italians can be measured, weighed and compared. (*De vulgari eloquentia*, ed. and tr. Steven Botterill)

It is as a result of Dante's own writings, and Petrarch's and Boccaccio's later, that the nearest Italy has to a standard language today is Tuscan: they wrote in Tuscan, and wrote so well as to become models of how the Italian language might be used.

It was in the early years of his exile that Dante wrote his *Convivio* (*The Banquet*), a treatise which he intended to consist of fourteen of his poems accompanied by commentaries, all of them together providing a banquet of knowledge. Of the projected fifteen books only four were completed; we can only conjecture why, but there may be a hint in the method of the *Convivio*, which was to consider the poems carefully in their literal and allegorical senses, in a way that included but went far beyond literary criticism. Possibly Dante came to realize that his ambitious project of an encyclopedic treatment of human knowledge and understanding was better entrusted to fiction, and more precisely the verse epic which became *The Divine Comedy*. *Convivio*

The *Comedy* is generally thought to have been started in the early years of his exile; there is a tradition however, related by Boccaccio, that he had completed the first seven cantos of the *Inferno* while he was still living in Florence; these cantos were then found by someone who realized their quality and took them to Dino Frescobaldi, a well-known Florentine poet; he had them forwarded to Dante, living at that time in Lunigiana at the court of the Malaspina family, with a request that the work should be continued; thus encouraged, Dante did continue it. At least ninety-three of the hundred cantos were composed during his exile. *The Divine Comedy*

It is impossible to summarize the contents of any of Dante's works and still remain fair to their quality, and this applies most of all to *The Divine Comedy*, which is possibly the greatest literary work ever produced in Europe. With that caveat in mind, it can be safely said that the poem opens in the year 1300, when Dante was middle-aged and suffering what might now be called a mid-life crisis, astray in an allegorical dark wood and unable to find the right path to lead him out of it. He is helped by the shade of Virgil, who reveals that he has been sent by Beatrice, who is now herself in heaven. Dante's rescue is represented as a journey which he has to make through the three realms of the afterlife – Hell, Purgatory and Heaven. Since the purpose of the journey is to show him the true nature of existence and thereby bring him to his senses, the physical details of it are allegorical; but these details – the geography of the realms he visits, the appearance and characters of the people he meets, his interaction with them and with Virgil – are all presented in physically realistic terms. It can be a mistake to read the poem with an obsessive eye for allegory. Often it seems best to take it as a literal fiction and allow the allegory to impinge on us in its own various ways. Dante has to scramble down into Hell, he has to climb up Mount Purgatory, and he has to float into space to get to Heaven: the significance of those movements is obvious. As with any long work, there are places where scholars may wrangle, and any reader may at times be baffled, but generally the point of what happens is crystal-clear. Dante himself, the protagonist, is seen time and again as a representative of the whole human race. The shades he meets are both sharply individualized and also generalized, in that they are actors in human history in all its untidiness while at the same time they embody sins and virtues which have their consequences in the realms where history no longer happens. Perhaps the most dramatic book is Purgatory: the souls there are striving to rise out of it, while those in Hell cannot change their place, and those in Heaven would not wish to. However, there is no lack of drama anywhere in the *Comedy*. In the face of such a powerful work it is needless to ask (although some have done so) whether it can be appreciated by a reader who does not share Dante's beliefs and presuppositions. Do we need to approve of human sacrifice in order to appreciate Homer? Or be an ancient Roman imperialist in order to enjoy Virgil? The drama of the *Comedy* is the same drama that is in the world around us here, but with its consequences brought home to us.

Select Bibliography

Editions of works by Dante Alighieri:
La Divina Commedia, ed. Natalino Sapegno, 3 vols. (Florence: La Nuova Italia, 1985)

La Divina Commedia, ed. Umberto Bosco and Giovanni Reggio, 3 vols. (Florence: Le Monnier, 2002)

The Divine Comedy, tr. Allen Mandelbaum (London: Everyman, 1995)

The Divine Comedy of Dante Alighieri, tr. Robert M. Durling, 3 vols. (Oxford: Oxford University Press, 1996–2011)

The Banquet, tr. Christopher Ryan (Saratoga, California: Anima Libri, 1989).

Monarchy, and Three Political Letters, trs. D. Nicholl and C. Hardie (London: Weidenfeld & Nicolson, 1954)

New Life, tr. J.G. Nichols (London: Hesperus Press, 2003)

Rime, tr. J.G. Nichols and Anthony Mortimer (London: Alma Classics, 2009)

De vulgari eloquentia, ed. and tr. Steven Botterill (Cambridge: Cambridge University Press, 1996)

Further Reading:

Anderson, William, *Dante the Maker* (New York: Crossroad, 1982)

Auerbach, Erich, *Dante, Poet of the Secular World* (Chicago, IL: Chicago University Press, 1961)

Boccaccio, Giovanni, *Life of Dante*, tr. J. G. Nichols (London: Alma Classics, 2010)

Boyde, Patrick, *Dante Philomythes and Philosopher* (Cambridge: Cambridge University Press, 1981)

Foster, Kenelm, *The Two Dantes and Other Studies* (Berkeley, CA: University of California Press, 1977)

Jacoff, Rachel, ed., *The Cambridge Companion to Dante* (Cambridge: Cambridge University Press, 1993)

Lansing, Richard, ed. The Dante Encylopedia (London: Routledge, 2010)

O'Donoghue, Bernard, *The Courtly Love Tradition* (Manchester: Manchester University Press, 1982)

Reynolds, Barbara, *Dante* (London & New York: I.B. Tauris, 2006)

Toynbee, Paget, *A Dictionary of Proper Names and Notable Matters in the Works of Dante* (1898), rev. Charles Singleton (Oxford: Oxford University Press, 1968)

Singleton, Charles, *An Essay on the Vita Nuova* (Cambridge, MS: Harvard University Press, 1949)

Williams, Charles, *The Figure of Beatrice* (London: Faber and Faber, 1943)

ALMA CLASSICS

ALMA CLASSICS aims to publish mainstream and lesser-known European classics in an innovative and striking way, while employing the highest editorial and production standards. By way of a unique approach the range offers much more, both visually and textually, than readers have come to expect from contemporary classics publishing.

LATEST TITLES PUBLISHED BY ALMA CLASSICS

To order any of our titles and for up-to-date information about our current and forthcoming publications, please visit our website on:

www.almaclassics.com